The Mass in My Life

The Mass in My Life

Cries of the Heart in the Prayers of the Mass

ROSEMARY LUNARDINI

iUniverse, Inc.
New York   Bloomington

iUniverse books may be ordered through booksellers or by contacting:

iUniverse
1663 Liberty Drive
Bloomington, IN 47403
www.iuniverse.com
1-800-Authors (1-800-288-4677)

The views expressed in this work are solely those of the author
and do not necessarily reflect the views of the publisher, and the
publisher hereby disclaims any responsibility for them.

978-1-4401-0979-9 (sc)
978-1-4401-0980-5 (ebook)

Printed in the United States of America

iUniverse revision date: 12/19/2008

"Will you come and follow me
If I but call your name?
Will you go where you don't know
And never be the same?
Will you let my love be shown,
Will you let my name be known,
Will you let my life be grown,
In you and you in me?"

John L. Bell

TABLE OF CONTENTS

PREFACE

Twenty-Eighth Sunday in Ordinary Time
Gospel of Luke 17:11-19

"Jesus, Master! Have pity on us!"
These are the words of ten lepers who stand a distance away from Jesus and call out to him. Jesus tells them to present themselves to the priests, a sign that upon their arrival they will be found clean. When this happens, only one returns and falls at the feet of Jesus in gratitude. Jesus asks, "Where are the other nine?"

Today my pastor Father Kevin said in his homily that we all experience not being thanked for gifts we give and things we do for people. When I receive a gift, someone has gone out of his way to do something just for me—something he did not have to do. When the giver is God, my gifts are my life, my loves, my beautiful world—as well as my faith in him who is the giver.

These are moving words of Jesus in the Gospel today: "Ten were cleansed, were they not? Where are the other nine?" Jesus even links the one leper's gratitude with his faith: "Stand up and go; your faith has saved you." Perhaps the initial faith of all of the lepers that Jesus could help them is not complete in the nine, for in them the expression of gratitude is missing. It is almost unthinkable that faith would not have this response of gratitude to the giver and the healer who is Jesus Christ.

As I hope to embark on a memoir of my experience of the Mass, I think a primary reason is gratitude for having the Mass in my life. It is at Mass that I kneel in the presence of God so often. This morning I think, as I often do, of what it is like to hear together with others the word of God and the homily of the priest. I feel that I am not on my own. The experience of Mass is both very public and very private. I say the same prayers, sing the same hymns, go to Communion a certain way as everyone else. I am linked with them in this formality of worship, although we each have our own thoughts and cries of the heart, each his own experience of grace. In this book I want to explore especially the experience that has been my own, bearing in mind that it is always united with others.

One constant of the Mass is this presence of other people. I see those who are carried in the arms of their parents and those who are wheeled in by helping hands. Those who come alone and those who, with their families, take up a whole pew. I can sense their experience as well as my own. I can see and hear their prayer, and this is very powerful. God works in part through my senses, and in the Mass I respond to what I see, hear, and touch. My heart goes out to young parents who are trying so hard to teach their children about God, to the middle-aged who are praying their children will return to Mass, and to the old for whom just being there is almost a miracle.

The priest, servers, and cantor are on the altar. My friends are all around me. My husband is next to me. Their presence leads me to love them and want to put things right if I have offended them or if they have offended me. Christ tells us explicitly to make peace with others before we present ourselves at the altar.

I pray for those who are here and for those who are not. Those who are at Mass elsewhere in the world, including most of my children and grandchildren and cousins. We take part in the same offering—this Sacrifice of the Mass. Those who are no longer on this earth are part of it too. I pray for those loved ones with whom I attended Mass through the years, especially my parents who were the first to bring me to Mass, along with my brother and sister. In the memory of my soul, Mother is still singing beautifully at Mass and Dad is doing his best, a little flat but always fervent.

Rosemary Lunardini
October 10, 2004

With gratitude to my husband, Virgil, who encouraged me to write this book and helped with technical details, and to Anne Allen, Sheila Brandes, and Gertie McGlinchey for reading the manuscript. I am grateful for Des Hudson's interest and the use of his photo of the Agnus Dei in stained glass.

PREPARATION

Feast of the Solemnity of Mary
January 1, 2005

On a dismal morning that seems like a springtime mud day rather than New Year's Day in New Hampshire, my husband and I walk the five blocks from home to Mass. The Mass for me is always, always beautiful and inspiring, but this special feast day always catches me up. I half-expect it to be about New Year's Day, but it is in fact devoted to the Motherhood of Mary. This observance in honor of Mary at first seems superfluous so soon after Christmas, for we have been celebrating the birth of Jesus, mindful of his Mother, for the past week.

Mass begins as the priest approaches the altar, and I am invariably reminded of the words of the *Introibo* of my childhood. When I was very young, the priest, standing at the foot of the altar, bowed low and said the Latin prayer in a voice that I could just hear:

"Introibo ad altare Dei"—"I will go in to the altar of God."

And then the altar server responded:

"Ad deum qui laetificat juventutem meam"—"To God the joy of my youth."

The older I get, the more I think of this prayer—think of God as the joy of my youth, always turning me back to the wonder of new eyes and ears and a mind fresh and sinless.

In his greeting, our pastor points out how blessed we are to be here in this church at this Mass today. In another part of the world a week ago a hundred thousand people lost their lives in a tsunami. Our prayers today are for them and for the survivors of that ocean wave which is impossible for me to imagine as I sit here in the security, serenity, and comfort of the church. I wonder what the

Mass will open up to me that I might not think of on my own about such immense loss of life in the face of one of nature's uprisings. Is God present in the tsunami? Why do the innocent suffer? Is prayer heard in the crash and sucking out of the wave?

Now, the first prayer and action of the priest and the people together is one that begins all Catholic prayer—the Sign of the Cross:

"In the name of the Father, and of the Son, and of the Holy Spirit."

The priest then blesses us:

"The grace and peace of God our Father and the Lord Jesus Christ be with you."

A blessing is so special that coming to Mass would be worth it alone. A few minutes later we hear today's reading from Numbers 6:24-26 in which God tells Moses how to instruct the priest to bless the people. He is to say:

"The LORD bless you and keep you!

The LORD let his face shine upon you, and be gracious to you!

The LORD look upon you kindly and give you peace!"

World events, feast days, personal lives be what they may, the Mass reminds me that I come together with these other people in the name of God and that we receive his grace and peace through the person of the priest in words taken from the Old Testament blessing. God blesses *me* always for my very self, even as he blesses all these *others* here, whoever they may be, for their very selves. The individuality, as well as the generality, of the blessing appeals to me and leads me to bow before God's blessing on others, as well as myself: If God blesses them, I bless them.

And so some things are unchanging, no matter the day or my mood. Whether it is a day of nothing momentous; the feast of a great saint; a day of wedding or baptizing or burying; or a day to remember the victims of a tsunami, the Mass calls me to become calm and to surrender myself, just as it begins. Today I need to surrender any Job-like questions that I think I can answer on my own, as well as my own ideas about the seeming redundancy of this feast day. I make a commitment. I will send forth my own voice in surrender, hope and praise with all these other people present.

The first major prayer is the *Gloria* of heavenly praise:
"Glory to God in the highest,
and peace to his people on earth.
. . .

For you alone are the Holy One,
you alone are the Lord,
you alone are the Most High,
Jesus Christ, . . ."

In the midst of the *Gloria* I begin to think that God *must* be present in the tsunami. He must be always present to his creation. Although this is not the first nor the last time I shall mull over this question, I do believe that at Mass we approach the divine realm, perhaps as Job did toward the end of his struggles when he admitted to God that there were things too awesome for him to understand. At the outset, God has pledged his peace to us in the priestly blessing and in the angelic *Gloria,* and that means something. Today it means that I hear again his promise of peace and believe in it, even for those whose lives were beaten and battered and sucked from them by a nature that had always sustained them.

Walking the few blocks home after Mass with Virg seems to be a good time to talk over my idea of writing a book about the Mass. Since retiring as a medical writer and editor, I have completed a longtime plan of organizing about a hundred of my parents' letters to me and writing commentaries on them. Gathered into my first book, *Book of Letters,* their words are a reservoir of what is so familiar and yet almost forgotten. In them my parents express in their own words their strong personalities, an immense interest in my family, reminders of my duties to others, the importance of friendships, and many of their own examples of Catholic life. *Book of Letters* exists in a very limited edition of one copy, bound by my husband for my personal use.

These letters written over thirty years may have prompted me to take an even longer view of my present subject: a remembrance of the Mass through the course of my life. Besides my parents' letters, another wonderful resource has come to light: the missals I have used to pray the Mass, most of which were put aside as I grew up and as the Mass itself changed. I am confident that these missals will help revive my memory of the Mass. Even as I hold them in my hands and begin to look through them again, I become aware of what they meant to me. An added benefit to my endeavor is that the missals serve as an objective guide to what the Mass has been like through the years 1938 to 2008.

Later, at home, I look up the Gospel of Luke 2:16-21 which was read this morning, and I find something new about Mary. The familiar part is that the shepherds, having heard that first *Gloria* while in the fields watching their flocks, arrive at Bethlehem and find the infant lying in a manger as the angel said. Then the Gospel relates that the shepherds tell what they have witnessed in the fields and repeat the angelic announcement of the Savior's birth. I had never thought of the effect upon Mary and Joseph of hearing that others now know this secret. Now a heavenly host was celebrating the birth of her child and making it known to the world from the very beginning of his life. The Gospel tells us: ". . . Mary kept all these things, reflecting on them in her heart."

Memory. Reflection. Cries of the heart. Mary used her own human powers to the fullest, so that all her life she would follow God's will. Thus she is a perfect source of inspiration as I begin to write of these reflections of my own heart, and I pray for the guidance of the great Mother of God, Mary most holy.

1

JOY OF MY YOUTH

"I will go in to the altar of God: to God, the joy of my youth."
Introibo
Saint Joseph Sunday Missal, 1953

My earliest memories of Mass go back to the age of six, when I was chosen to be one of four angels who led the second graders in their First Communion procession from the school to the small limestone church of Our Lady of Victory.

As an angel I had a close look at the class before me on their special day: the girls in white dresses with cap-held veils and the boys in white jackets and short pants, all holding their new prayer books and rosaries as they walked to the church. At the well-rehearsed right moment, we angels led them up to the altar rail and watched from the side as each in turn lifted a little head when the priest approached with the golden chalice.

Their prayer books fascinated me. The girls' book had a white cover with a picture of Mary holding a lily and watching over a little girl at her First Communion. A ray of light shone from beyond the chalice and over it, onto the girl's face. I looked forward to having one of these books the next year.

I had gone to Mass with my father, so I was told, for the first three years of my life. My parents often said that I (their only child at the time) then began to ask why my mother did not go with us. This was evidently too much for Mother. She herself told me often in my childhood that she became a Catholic so that I would have both of my parents "going to church together." I remember much talk of Mother going to instructions.

In her class of converts were two women who would become her friends. One of these was Dora, who like Mother was married to a Catholic man and had children about my age. As a woman with a job outside her home, she always made time for us on weekends. I loved Dora who always made us waffles before my mother had a waffle iron. The other woman was Betty, and we all were impressed with the story of the conversion of her entire family—the parents and four children. As my mother's conversion was such a big thing, it had to be an even bigger thing that a whole family became Catholic at the same time! About ten years later, Betty's husband sent us a copy of his newly-published book about St. Francis, and then a few years later a bouquet of flowers from them arrived at our house on a day of great sadness. Betty and Mother were not closest friends, but I believe they always remembered the steps they had taken together in becoming Catholics.

Mother loved and admired Dora in so many ways—yet she thought her friend was wrong a few years later to take her two daughters out of our school because the teacher would not allow one of them to wear a sweater over her uniform, a navy skirt and white middy blouse. Mother seemed to think that Dora may have been looking for a reason to do this, even though Mother also considered it foolish that a child not be allowed to wear a sweater if she was cold in school.

The sweater incident lived on in my mind for years, and I unwittingly learned—almost absorbed—something about it from Mother. I believed that she thought her friend had reservations about being a Catholic, since the education of one's children in a Catholic school was of great importance. Such a "revolt" was unusual. We all remained friends, but something was missing now that my best friends went to another school. I was glad that my mother would not do that to me, take me away from my Catholic school and my anticipated First Communion with my class—even though I was somewhat unhappy at school. As long as I had to go to school, I wanted it to be this school.

And so my mother through an unselfish act became a Catholic who loved being a Catholic. She continued to learn more through the years in a parish study group. I cannot remember a time she did not go to "study group." Even as she had a full life in the church, she kept a place in her heart for the Protestant faith of her own youth.

When we went South every summer to stay several weeks with her family, we attended the Methodist church on the road in front of the family home. My grandfather had been a Methodist preacher, but my grandmother was a Baptist—leading to a mixed marriage of sorts. As Mother's father died when she was only five, the youngest of his fourteen children from two marriages, she was mostly brought up in the Baptist church by her mother—although from my vantage point there was not a lot of difference. Many years later when I returned to the town, I found the Methodist church as I remembered it, especially the steps that led downstairs to Sunday School where the children had sung children's hymns, heard bible stories, and drawn pictures—church activities that had been utterly strange to me.

In my experiences with Protestant Sunday school, it seemed that all the children in town were there and so there must not be any Catholics. That was actually quite true. There were none. Back home, I had categorized about half my neighborhood friends as Protestants simply because they were not Catholics. However, few of them went to Sunday school. I learned early that Protestants did not have to go to church on Sunday as Catholics did; nevertheless, my childlike idea of a *good* Protestant was much like my idea of a *good* Catholic— someone who went to church on Sunday. After all, there was the third commandment God gave to Moses, "Remember to keep holy the Sabbath Day," which I thought must apply to them as well as to us. Although I had this shared Christian observance with these Protestant children on Sunday mornings in this Southern town, I felt like a misfit. At some point the children would come upstairs to join the adults, and I would take a seat next to Mother who obviously enjoyed being back in her old, familiar surroundings.

At first, I was only uneasy due to the strangeness, but later as I got into my formal Catholic education I had the distinct idea that I should not be going to that Protestant church. At an early age I knew what was missing: A priest giving people Holy Communion—bread they believed was really the body of Jesus. What would these Sunday school children think about that? Probably that it was very strange.

Mother seemed happy to be in the church of her own upbringing, singing the Protestant hymns she often sang around our house when she was working—hymns like "What a Friend I Have in Jesus" and "The Old Rugged Cross." Seeing her eyes fill with tears, I thought she must be sad for Jesus on the Cross, yet sad for some reason of her own.

I am sure that growing up Catholic and "going to church"— which meant the same thing as "going to Mass"—would not have been so wonderful for me without my mother's presence. She—and my father, of course—believed that she had made the right decision, and I was aware from an early age of the story of her conversion. It was done for me, it made me happy, and she was happy about it.

By the second grade I was learning that Jesus was on the altar as a victim, but in times past priests had offered animals to God. Jesus was the perfect victim because he was the Son of God. He offered himself to the Father (who was still in heaven) to make up for our sin. But there was more. At the Last Supper of his life, he called bread his body and wine his blood, and he told the apostles to do what he did when he changed bread into his body and wine into his blood. He made the apostles to be priests. So although he sacrificed his own life once, he wanted the priests to do it again and again in memory of him.

I learned that the Sacred Host which I would receive at my First Holy Communion was made of flat bread, because the Israelites of the Old Testament fled their homes in Egypt in such haste to escape the Pharaoh that they took with them unrisen bread for their long journey. And even after that bread was gone, they had manna, a miraculous bread, during the years they lived in the desert.

I worried about how I was going to swallow this bread—since it was actually the body of Jesus after the priest had said the words of Jesus over it. We were not to bite into it; rather we should let it melt on our tongues. As I watched older children carefully that year, the Host did not look to me like something that would melt.

Religion class in the second grade was devoted to the sacraments of the Holy Eucharist and Penance, since we would have our first confession shortly before our First Communion. Then there were the other preparations for the special occasion both at school and at home. Everything must be faultlessly done. It might have become a fearsome thing, exactitude overwhelming any joy, but that is not my memory. Exacting preparations meant that everyone knew what to do. I *was* nervous but when the big day came at last, and when I received the Sacred Host and it actually did melt on my tongue within a minute, I was very relieved. That day our class said the "Prayer before a Crucifix" after Communion.

This was found in the white prayer book titled *Pray Always,* and I now had my own copy. For me the tiny, gold, three-dimensional crucifix embedded in its own small alcove inside the front cover of the book was what I most loved about the book. The prayer is on the first printed page, facing the cross. If I had to choose one icon for my life, it would be this book with its secret crucifix made of white and gold paper. Whenever I come across the book I have to open it, for there inside is something like my own chapel contained in the cover that itself measures only 2-1/2 x 4 inches. It is perfectly designed for a child to read while looking upon the crucifix. The "Prayer Before a Crucifix" certainly has many big words for a second grader, but I dutifully said it anyway.

"Behold, O kind and most sweet Jesus,
I cast myself on my knees in thy sight,
And with the most fervent desire of my soul,
I pray and beseech thee that thou wouldst
Impress upon my heart lively sentiments
Of faith, hope, and charity,
With true repentance for my sins,
And a firm desire of amendment,
While with deep affection and grief of soul
I ponder within myself and mentally contemplate
Thy five most precious wounds;
Having before my eyes that which David spoke
In prophecy: 'They pierced my hands and my feet;
They have numbered all my bones.'"

The last two lines always gave me something to think about after Holy Communion. I wasn't certain who David was, but I did know whose hands and feet were pierced.

2

WHITE FOR JOY, BLACK FOR MOURNING

"Dominus vobiscum."
"Et cum spiritu tuo."
Saint Joseph Sunday Missal, 1953

The language of color is one that speaks to all ages, even the very young who usually learn colors before they do letters. I always was interested in what color the priest wore on any given day. I knew what the colors signified, because we had learned them in school. One favorite section of my prayer book describes the principle things needed for Mass and the garments that the priest wears.

All of these things appealed to me—the crucifix; the chalice, and its veil (always the same color as the priest's chasuble, or outer vestment, on any given day); the paten, a small gold plate; and the bell. The priest, who we school children sometimes glimpsed in preparation as we filed past the sacristy door to enter the church, dressed in the long white alb held by a cord, a stole crossed over his chest, and the chasuble. Most days, the outer vestments were green, the color symbolizing hope. White was frequently the color of the day: It symbolized joy. Black was the color of mourning, and purple of penance. Red signified the fire of love for God and was the color used on feasts of the Holy Spirit, who appeared to the apostles in fiery tongues over their heads; and feasts of the martyrs, who shed their blood for love of God.

These things of physical beauty and spiritual meaning I learned existed to glorify God and to be pleasing to him. The entire physical setting attracted the senses of children. The lighting of the high candles by the altar servers signaled the beginning of Mass, and the candles in turn illuminated vases full of flowers on the altar as gradually the church filled up with people.

I wished that other children in my neighborhood, those with whom I usually played, could go to Mass too. I thought they were missing something big. Early on, I learned that Mass was the same thing as Jesus' death on the cross; that he still, in some mysterious way, offered himself for our sins, even though he had redeemed us long ago. It was not hard to see that people still sinned, so I accepted that the Mass was still necessary for us. I also learned that at Mass I should pray in four ways: to praise God, thank him for his gifts, be sorry for my sins, and ask him to fill my needs.

There was also a certain fear of hellfire if I missed Mass. Hell, I imagined, must be something like the monstrous coal-burning furnace in the basement of our first home, an apartment house on Ashland Avenue. My father took care of the furnace, and sometimes as he opened the door to throw in more coal, I got a glimpse of actual flames or red-hot coals.

But with my parents, I was not likely to miss Mass. Even when traveling, we managed to find a Mass on Sunday, and by an early age I had quite a list of places we had attended Mass, from a lovely seminary on Lake Wawasee in Indiana, where my cousins spent summers, to a seamy old movie theatre on a beach in South Carolina.

How could I not love Mass when I had my First Communion prayer book to explain it and to give me simple prayers to say? The book's main part consists of illustrations of the actions of the priest on the left page, and the child's instructions and prayers for following the Mass on the right page. For example, for the prayer called the *Confiteor*, the illustration shows the priest bowing low before the altar, while the child is directed to kneel at this time and say this prayer:

"Dear Jesus, I am a sinner. But I wish to offer this Mass to make up for my sins and to get the help I need to keep out of sin after this."

I did not doubt that I sinned—impudence, anger, and envy of other children.

At the reading of the Epistle, the priest is shown reading from his Mass book while the child prays:

"Dear Jesus, make me glad to learn more and more about Thee. Help me to understand my Catechism and the sermons that are preached to us by the priests. Never let me give up my religion and lose Thee forever."

I could understand my Catechism better than the sermons preached by the priests. I pretty much ignored the sermons—probably because I was tested on the Catechism every day but never quizzed on the sermons. Also, I favored the written to the spoken word in learning most things. Spoken words often escaped my daydreaming kind of mind.

The Consecration—the changing of the bread and wine—is described as the holiest part of the Mass. The priest raises first the Sacred Host over his head for us to see, and we know now "It is really Jesus." When the bell rings, we look at Jesus and say, silently:

"My Lord and My God."

Then the priest bends over and changes the wine into the living blood of Jesus. . . . "It is really and truly Jesus Himself who is in the golden cup now." Again the bell rings, and again we pray:

"My Lord and My God."

These prayers seem very true to what I learned and believed about the Mass at a young age. At certain times in my life I have reached deep into a drawer for this little prayer book and found just what I needed—reminders of a child's faith.

In the next year or two, I graduated from my First Communion prayer book to the personal missal that most people, young and old, brought to church every Sunday. This was the *Saint Joseph Sunday Missal*. The key to using it was to know that the Mass was divided between the Ordinary part and the Proper part. The Ordinary never changed, but the Proper changed every day of the year. Preferably before Mass began, we looked up the day, month, and year in the liturgical calendar within the missal.

For example, if I arrived at Mass on a particular Sunday in May, I would have found that it was Pentecost and turned to the page on which the Proper for that day began. I needed to mark this page with a ribbon in order to turn back to it from the everyday prayers of the Ordinary.

The Proper included the prayer called the Introit (Wisdom 1:7):

"The Spirit of the Lord has filled the whole earth, alleluia; and that which contains all things has knowledge of the *voice*, alleluia, alleluia, alleluia";

The Epistle (Acts 2:1-11):

". . . And suddenly there came a *sound* from heaven, as of a violent wind blowing, and it filled the whole house where they were sitting";

And the Gospel (John 14:23-31):

" . . . the Advocate, the Holy Spirit, Whom the Father will send in My Name, He will *teach* you all things, and bring to your mind whatever I have said to you."

Voice. Sound. Teach. At the time, I surely did not recognize the linkages, or even the sources, of these prayers and readings within the Bible. I had no idea that at Pentecost, Mass began with an Old Testament prayer about the Spirit whose *voice* is contained in all things. I was more atuned to the first New Testament reading, in which Jesus promises that the Holy Spirit will come and *teach*; and to the second, in which the Holy Spirit appears in *sound* to the apostles. Even so, I was unaware that the apostles were celebrating the *Jewish* feast of Pentecost. I did know, because we were already anticipating Confirmation in the fourth grade, that the Holy Spirit comes in a completely unseen way to each person to give the strength, virtue, and wisdom to be holy. And certainly I knew why the priest wore red on Pentecost, that day when the apostles were set on fire with zeal to preach about Jesus.

The Proper of the Mass opened up the uniqueness of each day of the year—Sundays, weekdays, special observances and holy days. The holy days of obligation were the Circumcision of Jesus (January

1), the Ascension of Jesus (40 days after Easter), the Assumption of Mary (August 15), All Saints Day (November 1), the Immaculate Conception of Mary (December 8), and Christmas Day (December 25). The Proper of the Mass—containing most importantly the Epistles and Gospels—was our guide to the entire life of Christ as celebrated within our church over the liturgical year, from the beginning of Advent to the last Sunday after Pentecost.

In the early grades my class became very familiar with the unchanging Ordinary of the Mass. Our *Saint Joseph Sunday Missal* illustrated the movements of the priest and altar servers and contained Latin prayers on the left page and English prayers and instructions on the right. People could follow either one, or both to a certain extent, but the priest, who usually spoke in a low voice, said aloud in Latin at least the first words of most prayers. In this way, I picked up those Latin words as a key to knowing what the priest was doing. Along the way I learned some Latin, since its translation was on the facing page. Most people knew the *Gloria,* the *Sanctus,* the *Pater Noster,* and the *Agnus Dei,* as well as some short Latin prayers said by the priest and the responses said by the altar servers, or sung by the choir on behalf of the people. To a certain extent the people in the pews were bilingual at the Latin Mass, although we hardly realized it.

Most familiar among the short prayers was the *"Dominus vobiscum"* which means "God be with you." It was intoned frequently by the priest, followed by the response of the servers *"Et cum spiritu tuo,"* which means "And with thy spirit." This exchange between the priest and servers was first heard at the foot of the altar; then again when the priest kissed the altar after the Gloria and turned toward the people with his blessing. It also occurred before the Gospel, at the Offertory and Preface, and then in the final prayer. His *"Dominus vobiscum"* could not be missed, because he turned around to face us and then spread out his arms. This action was very special and dramatic in my childhood, when the priest mostly faced away from us, directing his prayers to the Father through Jesus Christ present in the tabernacle directly in front of him.

There were two other main divisions of the Mass to learn about—namely the Mass of the Catechumens and the Mass of the Faithful. I learned that in the early days of Christianity, the catechumens—those who wanted to become Christian but first had a period of initiation—attended only the first part of the Mass, leaving before preparations for the Eucharist began. I knew that people (my mother, for one) only received Jesus in Holy Communion after they were received into the Catholic Church.

It is amazing at what a young age my classmates and I learned about the Mass and even how to follow it in Latin. I knew this was properly a realm of some mystery that we entered in precise ways that came out of times long ago, times that went all the way back to Jesus. As we grew up saying about many things: "God can do anything," and "It is a mystery."

3

VIEW FROM THE CHOIR

"Kyrie eleison.
Kyrie eleison.
Kyrie eleison.
Christe eleison.
Christe eleison.
Christe eleison.
Kyrie eleison.
Kyrie eleison.
Kyrie eleison."

Saint Joseph Sunday Missal, 1953

By seventh grade, the girls of Our Lady of Victory were singing in the choir of our parish church. At a high Mass—that is, one that was sung—the *Kyrie* was the first chant. The priest began the first line of chant and we responded with the next line, continuing to alternate lines to the end. From the altar to the choir loft at the opposite end of the church, and back again to the altar, the voices of priest and choir answered each other across the expanse of the church, seeming to cover the people in this threefold prayer for mercy.

From the choir loft I had a new view of the church and the people. In the earlier grades, the girls had sat on one side of the church in the front pews, and the boys on the other side, each group with a Sister of Charity of Nazareth in attendance. So we had not sat with our families or special friends, but as we arrived for Mass one by one, we took the next available seat.

I was glad to escape from the front pews and climb the narrow stairs at the back of the church to the choir loft. There was a kneeler there, across the full width of the church, and as I said my prayers the whole scene unfolded.

The church itself was made of limestone from nearby quarries. The church and rectory, also of limestone, were perched on the edge of a deep, wooded ravine in the village of Marble Cliff. This was a small, secluded neighborhood wedged between Grandview and Upper Arlington on the outskirts of Columbus, Ohio. The entire complex of Our Lady of Victory—church, rectory, school, playground, sports field, and convent— covered about ten acres on Roxbury Road, all of it enclosed by a low, stacked limestone fence much like the one surrounding the homes on my own street a block away.

The limestone, originally thought to be marble—hence the name Marble Cliff—was all around us. A steep cliff behind the school and convent marked the boundary of our school playground. To me, it seemed like the edge of the world, but just beyond it were railroad tracks where, before our time, limestone excavated from the cliff and surrounding area was loaded aboard freight cars. This operation had been overseen by an Italian Swiss industrialist who built his home, later to be the convent, where he had a commanding view of his enterprise. Many years later, the land between our playground and the train tracks was cleared and made into a playing field—and, by then, fewer trains went by.

Roxbury Road had only four houses on it—one a white gingerbread-style house on the other side of the ravine, where my classmate Jan lived. My friend Gertie, who was Betty's daughter, lived at the corner in a turreted Victorian house. Across from it was the estate of the elderly owner of a downtown hotel. I crossed the property by entering one gate and coming out the other to get to and from school and church more quickly, all the time hoping Mr. Wallick would not be taking his daily walk. He seemed pleasant when any of us met up with him, but I always expected that someday he would tell us not to use his property anymore. I still remembered from earlier grades, an elderly man who stood like a stone statue in his yard as I passed by on my way to our former home, glaring at me as if to defy me to set a foot on his lawn. Mr. Wallick was not like that.

Across the street from Our Lady of Victory was a limestone mansion we walked by every day, never knowing who lived there, nor seeing anyone behind the thick shrubs. Later, it was sold and became St. Raphael Home for the Aged. For the first time we could go inside, to visit the residents, and some of us used to say that when *we* were aged, we wanted to live there. Only when George Bush (the first) ran for president and visited St. Raphael, recalling fond memories of visiting his grandparents who had built the house, did any of us learn that it had been the Bush home at least a generation before our time.

While some of the boys of our class were often on the altar serving Mass, we girls were singing the Mass. For a high Mass, the singing parts were the *Kyrie, Gloria, Credo, Sanctus,* and *Agnus Dei* interspersed with many short responses to the priests, as well as an Offertory hymn. For this, we frequently sang *"Panis Angelicus"*—"Bread of Angels." From the choir loft we looked out beyond the crossed rafters of the church to the white marble altar and Communion rail. On either side of these were two arched, limestone grottoes. On the left side, the grotto held a very natural and beautiful statue of Mary and the child Jesus; and on the right side, the grotto held a statue of St. Joseph. Votive candles by the statues of Mary and Joseph, as well as the large sanctuary lamp, were always lighted.

The church was enlarged about the time I graduated from high school—several pews were added in the front of the church and the sanctuary was pushed farther out. Behind the new placement of the altar was installed a twelve-foot-high mosaic of Mary and the Christ Child. Both Mary and Christ were depicted wearing crowns, with the Child standing atop a star-studded globe. The enormous panel of tiny pieces of blue, white, and gold ceramic tiles had been ordered for our church by our pastor Father Favret during one of his trips to Italy and installed by an Italian family who were parishioners. The mosaic was then and still is the loveliest work of art I have seen in a parish church in the United States. Large though it is—and the church is still fairly small—it is magnificent, drawing every eye to the altar and leaving no mistake that this is the church of the gentle woman who is Our Lady of Victory.

The effect was achieved, because there was not a lot of other religious art to command our attention during Mass. The mosaic, the white altar, the limestone arches and grottoes, wooden rafters, and chandeliers that looked medieval were the main features of the church—and these were altogether a wonderful sight from the choir.

My view of all the people there, looking down upon the pillbox hats of the women and the bare heads of the men, revealed many families who were our friends and others who were familiar only because I saw them at Mass all the time. There was always Joe, the sacristan, usually up front helping the priest in some way before or after Mass. My Dad said that Joe had been away from the Church for a very long time and so went to Mass daily to make up for all the Masses he had missed. I tried to imagine what the number of misses might be.

Most of the families were composed of mother, father, and three or four children. Many families had four to six—and one had thirteen. In about three families, I knew that the parents were divorced, and it was the mother who came with her children; but in others, the husbands were either not Catholic or not practicing Catholics.

I was always curious as to why some children came to church alone, or for that matter not regularly themselves, even when they attended a Catholic school. The largest group of these was the Italians. Now there were Italians who did come to Mass, but I remember that they always turned out for events like the May Procession. Later, I heard that Italians had a distrust of the church in their native country. Or they simply distrusted all authority—that was another given reason, although I never had any sympathy for any of these reasons or even knew if they held any truth. Much later, I learned that the Italians had met with some resistance from the first pastor who believed they should attend the Italian church in the nearby village of San Margerita where there was a community of Italians working in the quarries. Others among them, however, got along fine with the pastor.

The Donovans were one of the Irish families who were well represented. Everyone knew from the start that one of them, probably my classmate Michael, would have a religious vocation.

15

This family attended daily Mass, almost an absolute sign of a devout Catholic, and Michael, we used to say, already knew as much about saying Mass as the priest did. At times we saw him whisper to the priest during Mass, as if to remind him of something he might have forgotten to do.

In my own family, there were three children: my brother John, four years younger, and my sister Julie, ten years younger than I. From the choir loft, I could see my parents in a pew below with my little sister and, frequently, Johnny on the altar as a server. The boys were chosen to serve if they had an aptitude for learning Latin and were reasonably well behaved and dependable.

We girls were in the choir whether we could sing well or not. Besides singing on Sundays, we sometimes left school in the morning to sing a funeral Mass at the church. The music was somber, especially the Sequence *Dies Irae*. I was fond of singing, as dramatically as I could manage, the *Dies Irae* in Gregorian chant. It was splendid and moving for the funeral Mass of a Catholic. I believed that the dead person, who I frequently knew, had our prayers to help him gain eternal life. Those who had died were part of the Communion of Saints of which we heard much in school. We the living, if in grace, were also a part of it. I came to think of the Communion of Saints as a *choir,* with the voices of the living and the spirit voices of the dead lifted to God, all for one another, in their praise of him.

Of course funerals are also for the living, and the *Dies Irae* prompted me to think about the day of judgment. I had a sense of the meaning rather than an exact knowledge of the words of this chant. This is the translation of the first two verses:
"Nigher still and still more nigh
Draws the day of prophecy,
Doomed to melt the earth and sky.
Oh, what trembling there shall be
When the world its Judge shall see
Coming in dread majesty."

On any Sunday of the year, the *Agnus Dei* was my favorite part of the Mass to sing:
"Agnus Dei, qui tollis peccata mundi, miserere nobis.
Agnus Dei, qui tollis peccata mundi, miserere nobis.

Agnus Dei, qui tollis peccata mundi, dona nobis pacem."

In English, this is:
"Lamb of God, who takes away the sins of the world, have mercy on us.
Lamb of God, who takes away the sins of the world, have mercy on us.
Lamb of God, who takes away the sins of the world, grant us peace."

The *Agnus Dei* has a restraint about it, which heightened my appreciation of it. In this prayer sung just before Holy Communion, Jesus is the Lamb of God, a pure victim. I both experienced myself and witnessed from the choir loft, a change in the people. This was not the time for a hearty *Gloria*, but rather for the gentle, repetitive words that change to "grant us peace" at the very end.

The choir loft was also a good place to observe people going to and returning from Holy Communion. I was very interested in who was with whom, what the other girls wore, and how devotional they were. Although we girls often tried to get each other to laugh, at Holy Communion we were perfectly serious. At last, after everyone else had received, the choir filed down the stairs and went to Holy Communion. Our organist was always the very last person to go to Communion. Nancy played the organ while everyone else received, so that she had just enough time to get down the stairs and up to the altar rail herself. She was a classmate who was exceptional in every way—brilliant in all studies, talented in music and dance, strong in sports, fun loving, and she seemed to even have a spiritual maturity. I could not hold a candle to her; nor could any of us. There was no envy of Nancy, only awe that someone our own age was so accomplished. We also learned the important lesson that no life is perfect, for we knew that Nancy had a more difficult family life than the rest of us.

It was good to know the people. It was also good that I had my old standby "Prayer Before a Crucifix" to bring me back to thinking about Jesus.

4
Your Servant John

> "... bid your holy angels receive him and
> bear him to our home in paradise."
>
> Collect, Burial Mass
> *Saint Andrew Daily Missal*, 1956

During four years of college, new intellectual and social interests began to chip away at family and church as the center of my life. Although I lived at home, I came and went without paying much attention to my family, so important was my own life. I went to Mass at home or on campus and helped a sorority sister become a Catholic through the Newman Center. Everyone who knew me pretty much knew me as a Catholic, but few college friends in those days were Catholic like me. My support was gone, and I was found lacking.

A question, hardly formed, about being a Catholic came unexpectedly into my mind at times: "Is this what I always want for myself?" At times, I felt privileged to have a faith with a strict moral code. But other times, I didn't want guilt hanging over my head, with the necessity of confession staring me in the face. I might have continued deeper into this line of thinking until I gradually fell away from all the life-giving sacraments of the church—and abandoned the Mass itself.

But that was not to happen, and I think I know the reason.

A day came, on April 3, 1959, when my family would have to face the hardest day of our lives. A caller in the middle of the night told my father the horrible news that his son was dead. Johnny was killed in an auto accident after he, another boy, and two girls left a Dairy Queen. He was almost seventeen. My parents were so overcome by disbelief and grief that I could only try to hold my own somewhat apart from me for awhile, as if it didn't belong to me.

We were so distraught that I don't know how we got from home to Our Lady of Victory in the morning. Our assistant pastor, Father Johnson, who had come to the house in the early morning hours to offer comfort, now offered Mass for the soul of our Johnny. I kept thinking that we were all together here for Easter Sunday, just a few days ago, an early date for Easter. Christ had *already* died. Christ had *already* risen. How could Johnny be dead—*now?* How could my darling brother, the sweetest boy, be *dead?*

Now in this Saturday morning Mass a few hours after his death, his family was virtually lifted onto the altar with Christ to be exalted and consumed like him, like Johnny. For surely my parents gave their greatest gift that day—they sacrificed their first and only son.

Our neighbor Mr. Donovan, who was always at daily Mass, came over to my parents and said, "I remember seeing you all together here on Easter." Mr. Donovan usually didn't talk much to people, but that was a good thing for him to say, to remind us of Easter when we went to Mass together for the last time. It occurred to me how good it is that some people are at Mass *every* day. They are there when death comes into our midst, among the first to offer prayers for the dead and consolation to families. They are like divine messengers who are gathered at the Lamb's Supper, and they help in a different way than others who begin to gather around the bereaved. Later, at home, we received a bouquet of white flowers from my mother's friend Betty, and all of us were so moved by this gesture. Most people send flowers to the funeral home, but these white flowers in our living room seemed to evoke a sense of the presence of one who was not there.

Over the next few days, there were several more Masses. On Sunday morning, Mother, Dad, Julie and I went out to St. Charles Preparatory School where my brother was a student. We were led to the Lower Chapel, where Mass was sung by the seminarians. The chapel seemed to me as secretive and underground as a catacomb, and this Mass for a departed soul was unlike any I had witnessed. The voices within these vaulted walls were as those of a heavenly choir breaking through, so close and yet ethereal, as if heaven had already made this music its own and heaven had already taken Johnny for its own. All of this, and yet the gut-wrenching reminders of his death resurfaced anew each moment. I would be uplifted by some aspect of the Mass and feel better; then I would think that he was gone from us forever as we knew him, that he had died unfairly and too young.

Then came the day of his funeral at Our Lady of Victory, as the church filled with St. Charles students in ties and jackets. They were clean-cut and crew-cut like my brother. It seemed that he should still be there among his classmates and his football teammates as he had been when the team and parents were photographed at the fall banquet. Instead, my parents had his face in that photograph enlarged and framed, so that we could remember him as he was not long before he died.

In the choir loft, another class of students sang the same solemn high Requiem Mass that I had sung so many times. In the St. Charles school paper, an obituary noted that many students attended the funeral and the congregation joined with the choir in singing the *Kyrie, Sanctus,* and *Agnus Dei.* This was not the custom at the time and so merited a mention in the paper.

I must have had my *Saint Andrew Daily Missal* in hand to follow the Requiem Mass, and my father had a booklet titled, "The Rite for Christian Burial and the Funeral Mass," published by Liturgical Press in 1956. I realized this only on finding the little book among his keepsakes after he died, with a note— "from Johnny Murphy's funeral Mass." My father had written his son's name on it as if to say to later generations—*This is my son whom I loved. Do not forget him.*

The Introit at its very beginning in the Burial Mass was that most familiar Catholic prayer for the dead:

"Eternal rest grant to them, O Lord; and let perpetual light shine upon them."

The Collect followed, at its core a summary of Catholic belief and petition concerning the dead:

"O God, to whom it belongs to have mercy and to spare, we humbly entreat You for the soul of Your servant John, whom You have summoned today from this world, that You would not deliver him into the hands of the enemy, nor forget him forever, but bid Your holy Angels receive him and bear him to our home in paradise, so that since he believed and hoped in You, he may not undergo the pains of hell but may possess eternal joys. Through Christ our Lord."

The Gospel of John told the story of Martha at the death of her brother Lazarus:

". . . Jesus said to her: 'I am the Resurrection and the Life; he who believes in Me, even if he die, shall live; and whoever lives and believes in Me, shall never die. Dost thou believe this?' She said to Him: 'Yes, Lord, I believe that Thou art the Christ, the Son of God, who hast come into the world.'" (John 11:25-26)

None of this ritual was new to me. I had been steeped in it, gone through it with others, prayed it, sang it most of my life. Now was my family's time to come forward and, under the wings of the Church, bury our own loved one. At the same time, in two other Catholic churches across the city, two other families were burying their daughters. For on that night, not only Johnny but two girls— Rita and Jane—died in the crash. My brother's friend Michael was the only survivor.

I felt heartbroken that my parents had lost their only son and Julie and I our only brother. I also felt guilty that I myself was still alive. Wanting to help my parents and sister in their grief, which I knew would last a long time, probably forever, I turned to a friend whose brother had died in an explosion about a year before. "What can I do to help my parents?" I asked him. "Go to Mass," he said matter-of-factly. I felt like saying, "Is that it?" I knew we would do that.

In the days that followed I asked myself another question: "What change is needed in *me*?" I began to have the idea soon after Johnny's death that he had died for me. Johnny had just celebrated his risen Savior at Mass, at the altar of his youth, a few days before his own life was given up; and I, although present that Easter Sunday, had been on the verge of looking the other way.

My friend was right. Mass did help. I was grateful that it brought some calm to our souls, as we turned to the sacrifice Jesus made for our salvation. We were now so personally aware of being a part of it and we saw Johnny as an innocent victim, so like Christ in that way, that we *knew* he was taken to Jesus.

Soon after the accident, the three sets of grieving parents met each other for the first time. They visited, consoled each other, told each other about their children, and went to the many Masses that were offered for all of their children. Their consolation of each other never wavered through the years that followed, long after Julie and I left home. When my mother died more than twenty years later, my father wrote to me that he had been invited by Rita's parents to attend Mass for Mother at their church and to have dinner with them.

While this tragedy of losing their children brought the three grieving families together, my family could have done better in forgiving Michael than we did. He was so young, a new driver, and did not mean to cause harm to anyone. The four children were alive on a warm spring night and just beginning to date, to have that sense of being with someone special.

Mother's grief overwhelmed her at times. I am sure that in her heart when she prayed, she could approach forgiveness; but I believe that absolute, lasting forgiveness was harder to come by. For the rest of her life, anything could open the wound until she was ready for death. My father did better at this, or so I believe.

Rather than speak for my parents, I should look to myself. Did *I* forgive my brother's friend? Although I soon moved away and had little contact with the old neighborhood, did *I* care if he had a good life in all the years since that night? Did *I* pray for him and his family who were also devastated by this accident? I should not approach the altar of the Lord unless this is so.

After my father's death, I found in his papers this letter to him and my mother from a Dominican brother:

April 10, 1959

Dear Mr. and Mrs. Murphy,

Today in a letter from home the news came to me of your son's tragic death. Since I had the privilege of working with you, Mr. Murphy, . . . while a student at Notre Dame, and now as a fellow Notre Dame alumnus, I want to tell you both how sorry I am that God has taken your son from you in such a sudden and unexpected way.

You have this strength-giving consolation: your son is nearer to Our Lady now, than at any other time in his life. And being near to Our Lady, surely this is to be all the closer to her Son, Our Lord. But at the same time he is nearer to God, he seems farther away to you. And this is the cross Our Lord has given you. Your son is gone. But please remember that he has gone to see God, and this is the way God wants it. The acceptance of the will of Our Lord, in this is your peace and joy.

Remember, too, that Our Lady knew what it was to lose a Son. The whole theme of her life is summed up in her reply to the angel Gabriel: 'Be it done to me according to Thy Word.' Our Lady lived the meaning of those words, not only on the first Christmas, when she looked down at her divine Son resting in her arms, but on the first Good Friday, when she looked up to see Him dying on the arms of the Cross.

May Our Lord, then, give you the grace to bear this trial, as He would have you bear it: in Him, with Him, and through Him. This is the spirit of Mary, Our Mother, who wanted only the will of her Son, whether at Cana or Calvary. And this, as you know so well, is the spirit of Notre Dame.

Sincerely,
Brother Vincent

5

A New Table

"Your wife shall be like a fruitful vine
in the recesses of your home.
Your children like olive plants around your table."
Gradual, Nuptial Mass
Saint Andrew Daily Missal, 1956

My wedding at Our Lady of Victory a year and a half after my brother's death was the kind of happy occasion my family needed. Not only had I found the right man with whom to share life as I wanted it to be, my parents also soon came to love Virg. Mother thought he was very handsome and liked the way he became part of the family, while Dad was impressed that he was a Notre Dame graduate and football enthusiast like himself.

Virg was from a large Italian-Irish family in western Massachusetts, and he fit right into our stormy, competitive family pastimes of sports, games and cards. He also brought to us a love and knowledge of nature which was not our long suit. We all began to learn about birds, one of Virg's main interests.

Friends had introduced us because we were both Catholics. This was an especially thoughtful thing for college friends who were not Catholics themselves to do; and I cannot bear to think that, without them so many years ago, I might not have Virg in my life.

On the day of our marriage, standing for the first time in the sanctuary of Our Lady of Victory and giving our promises to each other, we did not know how soon sorrow would come upon us. I soon became pregnant and had no problems, but as I waited and waited, on the tenth day past the due date, our baby was stillborn. As I was awaking from anesthesia, the news was broken to me. I was confused. I could not understand that the baby was not inside me anymore (it had been there for so long); and then that the baby was outside of me, but it was *dead*. Virg, then Mother, were soon at my bedside, saying a little more about it, but the mind and heart on reentering a world so changed from its expectations can only take in so much. I was surprised to see my still-new husband's grief: Until then he had always seemed stoic to me, but now I learned two intimate things about him: how much he loves his first child and how death grieves him.

Outside my hospital room were all the sounds of hungry new lives and carts of clattering bottles of formula ready for those who were not breast-fed. When a nurse mistakenly came into my room with a bottle a *second* time, I had to shake my head a second time and say, "There's no baby here." But the next morning, I heard a faint, yet distinctive sound—a bell ringing out in the hall of the obstetrics ward at Mount Carmel Hospital, coming closer. Then it entered my room. I could see that a nurse rang the bell and that she preceded a priest who appeared to be bringing Holy Communion to *me*. The whole scene was like one I might have seen in an illustration of a book of saints, and I could not believe it was happening to me.

In those few days, no one at the hospital spoke to me about my dead baby. But every morning the priest came through the ward, and I waited as the bell stopped at other rooms, knowing it would stop at mine too. I was ready for it. On those mornings, Holy Communion was an exquisite experience of the Sacrament. I laid all my grief on my Lord.

No other maternity patient was put in the room with me, I surmised so as not to mix me closely with happy mothers and babies. The sadness was huge and as unexpected as Johnny's death had been. When I fell asleep, I had to relearn it all when I woke up, over and over. I knew at the outset that this loss was a lesser version by far than the one my parents had suffered; however, at times I felt I had lost everything for never having seen and held my baby. Virg, my parents, and my sister buried her in the Queen of Angels area of St. Joseph Cemetery, not far from my brother's grave.

Just as I was preparing to go home, someone from the hospital came by and said matter-of-factly that my baby had been baptized. I was nonplussed by the professional coolness, because the facts—

both the stillbirth and then the news of the Baptism—were so extraordinary to me. But I believed that in her Baptism, the sign of faith had been put upon our child as fully as if she had been able to live an earthly life and had accepted Jesus. She went right to Jesus.

Fifteen months later, the same hospital and doctor gave me extra attention as our son came into the world. We took little Virgil Joseph III for Baptism to the Newman Center, the Catholic student center near campus that was our own parish. Nearby our graduate student apartment was a World War II-era quonset hut, where priests from Newman said Mass on Sundays for married students. Often I brought the baby to Mass there by myself. I wondered what to do about my husband who had research or the everlasting dissertation to work on. However, when we moved to Potsdam, New York, he returned to Mass. And, of course, by then the dissertation was in fact finished and he had a real job. We joined Christian Family Movement and had a special sharing of faith with the other couples in CFM, mostly young faculty families who had moved to the college town from other parts of the country.

I will always remember one CFM couple who had six children including a newborn baby. In all of our discussions at CFM they were clearly very strong Catholics. One Sunday when there was a coffee after Mass, the husband offered to run to the store to buy more cream that was needed—this was typical of the man, always pitching in to help. That morning, on the way there or back, he suffered a fatal heart attack. I never felt so inept as the morning a couple weeks later when I went to visit my friend. I was no stranger to loss in life, but the loss of the young father of this large family was more than I could imagine. Seeing my friend come out of the shadows of her house into the kitchen, hearing the baby in another room, I was left almost speechless. I could say the usual things, but with a sense that my friend's faith exceeded my own.

For us, fifteen months after Joey, another baby was born. Sheila was a happy baby who smiled every time anyone came near her. There was simply happiness within her, I thought, for she was just the same after being put in a body cast from the waist down at the age of two months. This was done to correct congenitally dislocated hips. I spent her first summer at my parents' house where Mother helped me take care of these little ones and then in the fall when we returned home, Sheila's cast was removed for good.

Not quite two years later, Brenda was born in the midst of a North Country blizzard that closed roads just following our arrival at the hospital. I was sorely missing family help during these first years that I had ever lived away from my parents. On top of that, there was so much need, what with our rapidly growing family. Our CFM families and other neighbors were helpful to each other since we were all in the same boat, far from our families—and no one was in such need as the family that had lost its father.

As the prayer from our Nuptial Mass had said, our children were indeed "like olive plants around our table." They were our blessing, our wealth, our watchfulness, and our future, growing and learning so fast it left us breathless. Usually while the children napped I did some of the dinner preparations, so that when they awoke we could enjoy the late afternoon together, waiting to spring something new they had learned on Dad when he got home from work.

On those afternoons, we put on our records and had impromptu dancing and parades around the house. Everybody loved the album "Let's have a Parade," and I joined in as we got our metal pans and wooden spoons, taking turns as leaders of the parade. We also liked the Mamas and the Papas, especially their recording of "Sing for Your Supper." Having missed out on being a hippie, that slightly hippie, back-to-earth idea in the song appealed to me at the time, and I felt like we *were* singing for our supper on those late afternoons. And so we marched and danced and sang until I had to go back to the kitchen, and usually, right on the dot, Virg came in the door. Soon we all sat down at the table for dinner. There was a completeness about being at the table that time of day that always filled me with a sense of well being. Children rested. Dad home from work. Dinner ready. Grace said. Time to relax. Time to be all-together again. *Not* hippie.

Even though there was great enjoyment of family life in these years, I was in a rush for each child to advance to the next step—in other words, to grow up, although I didn't think of it in such harsh terms at the time. If one was crawling, I wanted him to be walking. If one was talking, I wanted her to be reading. As soon as they were old enough for nursery school, off they went. I don't know what the rush was all about, except that I wanted them to be successful kids! And they were! But they would have been anyway, in due time.

Part of the rush was about me, especially after they were in school all day. It was about what I was going to do next with my life. Although I really liked being a stay-at-home mother, society seemed to be pushing mothers to work outside the home. I was in a quandary: Should I begin to work now, part-time? Should I go back to school and become a teacher? Or a librarian? Or what? How I just wished I were a nurse! Many friends were nurses, and they worked one or two evening shifts a week.

One winter when I was homebound for three months with a persistent pneumonia, I rediscovered my original desire to write. For several years I continued writing every day, often going back to bed after everyone had left the house, since that was where I had gotten started in my writing life. A few stories were published, and they boosted my confidence. I still thought it a long shot that writing would ever really amount to anything professional for me. It took so much time and skill and paid so little. However, I was full of ideas to write about and the most driven to do it as I had ever been about anything. These years were my apprenticeship.

We had moved again, to Ottawa, Canada, in 1969 when Joe was six years old. Although Virg had been among the first lay readers at our Potsdam church about 1966, it was in Canada that we first experienced all the changes in the Mass following the Second Vatican Council. The Mass began to be spoken entirely in English, rather than in Latin, and Gregorian chant and Latin hymns soon gave way to English hymns and folk songs. The people now said aloud some of the prayers they had formerly read in their missals, and lay people became readers, Eucharistic ministers, and song leaders on the altar.

The priest began to face the people rather than the traditional altar where the tabernacle, housing the sacramental presence of Christ, had been the center of every church. A new table was centered in the sanctuary or the old altar was moved forward, so that both priest and people faced each other over it. From my place in the pews, there seemed to be a new problem with the presence of the tabernacle now *behind* the priest. In most churches, the tabernacle was removed from its central position to a reservation chapel, but often still within the sanctuary.

For our ten years in Ottawa, living in a brand new suburb, we attended Mass in a public high school gym with many hundreds of people from our community. I especially welcomed the English and French-language lay ministers, with all the people singing and praying aloud. I did still hold a hope that the very beautiful Latin Mass and our centuries of sacred music would not be forgotten.

There were advantages to the priest and people gathering around the table of the Lord, for the people to see all that the priest did and to respond to him, and for him to see and respond to us. Only later I felt the loss of a sacred sense of the people praying, albeit silently, *with* the priest as both of us faced in the *same* direction toward the cross, the altar, the tabernacle—towards God as it were. There was something to say for each way, but we now had only the new way.

The new table in the sanctuary focused on the Supper of the Lord. The Last Supper I have always thought of as a prelude to the sacrifice that follows it, by which Christ accomplishes what he has promised and shared with his friends at Supper. In this way, altar incorporates table.

Although I was participating in the Mass more in outward ways than previously, I did not follow it as closely. My old *Saint Joseph* and *Saint Andrew Missals,* from which I had learned and followed the Latin Mass, were of no use anymore. At first the missalettes, nicely provided for everyone, seemed so modern, so disposable. We could just throw them out when a liturgical season was over. My reaction to this innovation took time to develop, until finally I had to admit how much I missed the thin, tissue-like paper and expressive woodcuts of my very own missals, with every prayer of the Mass and explanations of every part of it.

Living in our suburb with Mass at the high school, my children never had a church that was a home to them, a refuge for prayer to stop in and talk to God as a friend, and a place to look at Jesus on the cross and know that he was present in the tabernacle. They never had a place of warmth and welcome, yet a soaring space that uplifted the spirit. They never served on an altar, nor sang in a choir. They never had a place like Our Lady of Victory.

Each child's First Communion was a moveable feast. The first took place in a distant church that was actually our parish church; the second in the church but with the children scattered about, sitting with their parents; and the third in the gym of their Catholic elementary school. The children dressed somewhat special, but there were no suits for the boys and no white dresses and veils for the girls. No prayer books. And no rosaries.

At the time I mostly saw the good things that came out of those days and only occasionally felt winsome for something that was no more. There was something to say for stripping down to the essentials: our priest; his chalice—an earthenware vessel; and the altar—a portable table covered with a hand-woven cloth, its movability a necessity in the high school gym. The choir was all of *us*—several hundred strong! If things I loved were missing, I learned that the Mass is always beautiful, always beneficial. Our whole family went gladly. We especially liked going to the Mass in French, and I guessed that French—a language we were all learning, but one that held an elegant element of the old mystery—took the place of Latin for us.

At times I remember our pastor, Father Soucy, a warm-hearted man, spreading his arms wide, saying to us:
"Le Seigneur soit avec vous."

And we said to him:
"Et vous aussi."

During these years I began turning to the bible oftentimes when I returned from Mass and wanted to read something I had heard there. Our family bible is the Confraternity edition, issued in remembrance of the Marian Year 1954, lavishly illustrated and with gold-edged pages. I treated it as an heirloom, although it was brand new when we received it as a wedding gift. We had first put it to use to find names for our daughters from its lists of saints' names, deciding on Sheila, the Celtic form of Cecelia; and Brenda, after the Celtic Brendan. I was faithfully entering births and Baptisms, then First Communions and Confirmations in its family history pages.

Our bible definitely had more to offer. I first became intrigued by the words of Jesus, which were printed in red type. In the beginning, I just sought out the words in red type. Among those that impressed me so much were his words in the beatitudes in Matthew 5:3: "Blessed are the poor in spirit, for theirs is the kingdom of heaven"; at the Last Supper in Luke 22:19: "This is my body which is being given for you; do this in remembrance of me"; and on the Cross in Luke 23:24: "Father, forgive them, for they do not know what they are doing."

Many others, unremembered now, I looked up either for clarification or simply because I wanted to read more of what I had heard at Mass. Just the act of looking into the bible was new. I knew the Christian story, but I was just beginning to bring it to life, and to bring it to the Mass in my life. For me, the opening up of the bible for the people to read, to study, and to know better was the best gift of the Second Vatican Council. And in that way as well, the Mass in my life changed before my eyes.

6

Words of Life

"Not as man sees does God see, because man sees the
appearance but the LORD looks into the heart."

First Reading, 1 Samuel 16:1-13
Saint Andrew Bible Missal, 1982

The baby steps I was taking into the bible were at first a response to the Scripture readings in the first part of the Mass, the most obvious bible-based part. The *New American Bible* of 1970 had become established as the Scriptural source for the readings in the Mass.

By this time a reading from the Old Testament had replaced the shorter Gradual. I loved the First Reading, because, combined with the responsorial psalm from the Old Testament and the Epistle and Gospel from the New Testament, it added to my knowledge of the whole bible. I began to find it interesting to connect the readings into a common theme, which I knew was present to a certain extent in their selection to be read together. This exercise often led to a better understanding of each of them, and together they could give a powerful lesson on any particular Sunday.

For example, on the Fourth Sunday during Lent one year in Cycle A of the readings, the First Reading was from I Samuel 16:1-13. In this reading, the Lord calls Samuel to go out and find the one he has chosen to be king from among the sons of Jesse. Samuel looks and looks for the chosen one as Jesse and seven of his sons come to the sacrifice. The Lord further orders Samuel:

"Do not judge from his appearance or from his lofty stature, because I have rejected him. Not as man sees does God see,

because man sees the appearance but the L ORD looks into
the heart."

And so God rejects the first seven sons before the youngest,
David, who is tending sheep, is summoned. They must not begin
the sacrificial banquet until he arrives. The Lord points David out to
Samuel, who anoints him with oil "and from that day on, the spirit
of the L ORD rushed upon David." The Lord looked into the heart
of David and found there what no other man could see. Perhaps
an openness, even a vulnerability to be filled with the spirit of the
Lord.

Certainly the choice of David would seem unusual, given that
he is known for his later sin with Bathsheba and the untimely death
of her first husband. Why would God in his all-knowingness choose
a man, subject to such weakness, to lead his people? Over the years,
paying closer attention to the psalms, I came to see David as one
with a deep and expressive love of the Lord, a musician whose joy
overflowed in songs of praise and longing that carry through the
centuries.

On this particular Lenten Sunday, the responsorial psalm by
David recalls his days tending sheep and points out his own chosen
shepherd:

"The L ORD is my shepherd, there is nothing I shall want."
Psalm 23:1

Samuel and Psalm 23 are beautiful examples of a sharing in
divine love. In the first case, the Lord chooses David, then David
chooses the Lord. The Lord, a king, chooses David, a shepherd, to
be a king; and in turn David, a shepherd, chooses the Lord, a king,
to be his shepherd. It is an astounding reversal of roles, each one
giving of himself to the other an identity that is his very own. Then
Psalm 23 presses home why a lowly shepherd is one chosen by the
Lord, and chosen by us, to fill all our needs.

The Second Reading of this Mass, the Epistle to the Ephesians
5:8-14 points out that people were once in darkness but now are
in the light of the Lord. We are to take no part in deeds done in

darkness. When we condemn them, "they are seen in the light of day." Paul writes:

"Awake, O sleeper,
arise from the dead,
and Christ will give you light."

This short epistle sets the stage for the Gospel of John 9:1-11 which tells the story of the man born blind, on whose account Jesus corrects his disciples for thinking that personal sin—probably his parents' sin—caused his affliction. Jesus says something so astounding:

"Rather, it was to let God's works show forth in him."

In words similar to the Epistle, the deeds of the Father are done in the light of day—but the night comes on. Jesus then tells his disciples that his time in the world to do the work of the Father is soon over. Jesus gives sight to the man born blind, and the man testifies to what Jesus has done for him. The Pharisees, who have witnessed the whole thing, throw the cured man out of the temple. The Gospel says that Jesus sought him out and asked him, "Do you believe in the Son of Man?" The man says, "I do believe, Lord."

Then Jesus says something else pretty amazing:

"I came into this world to divide it,
to make the sightless see
and the seeing blind."

The Epistle reverberates with those words of Samuel:
"Not as man sees does God see. . . ."

I see how David and the man born blind, each upon his anointing, receives the spirit of God. In the case of the blind man, Jesus himself smears mud over his eyes in a kind of anointing, as a sign of life-changing grace, which brings about his conversion in faith to Jesus. Jesus rebukes the Pharisees, who witnessed the healing. While they think they see, they are presented as the truly blind men in this account.

But the most enigmatic words of Christ are about the necessity of doing the works of God while it is still day, ending in:

"While I am in the world,
I am the light of the world."

In my early years of bible study, I grew up on the commentaries of William Barclay, a Scottish New Testament scholar who wrote the *Daily Study Bible Series*. I especially depended on Barclay to learn the background and explanation of each section of the New Testament. He also expressed theological insights along with his inclusion of many interesting cultural details. In the case of this Gospel of John, he notes that the miracles are always a sign of the glory and power of God; and that suffering and afflictions always are opportunities for displaying God's grace.

Surely the work of Christ, the Light of the World, is ongoing, but Barclay offers this: "God is always saying to us: 'Now is the time.' It is not that the power of Jesus grows less or that his light grows dim; it is that if we put off the great decision [to accept Christ as our Savior] we become ever less able to take it as the years go on."

It seems to me that in this Gospel Christ is also looking ahead to his passion and death. Then the powers of darkness will appear to have had the day. Facing up to human time, Christ presses on with his earthly mission, separating for people—the man born blind, his own disciples, the Pharisees, all who see and hear—the very real distinctions present in the world: He comes from God and is light. Sin lurks in darkness, as St. Paul reminds the Ephesians. In this way, in his teachings, Christ does indeed divide the world, separating light from darkness as in the creation of the world. And then by his victory over sin and death, he relights the Light of the World.

From these related readings, coming one right after the other as they did one day years ago during Lent, I see a new way of looking at sin in the New Testament. An important part of the story of the blind man is revealed when Jesus tells his disciples that sin did not cause the man to be born blind.

Jesus seems always interested in more than the physical healing miracles he performs. The lesson is not even about human eyesight! To truly see is to believe in the one who came as the Light of the World, in whom God's work is visible. To believe is to see. For the man born blind and for me.

Although my interest in the bible was whetted while my children were in elementary school, such formal opportunities to study the bible as I have just described arose when our family moved to Hanover, New Hampshire. I had already made a personal decision to be a more active Catholic at the parish level when I left Ottawa. In our years there, little was offered or asked from us by our parish— this in part because our "separate" school, essentially a public school with a Catholic curriculum supported by Catholic taxpayers, took care of the education of our children. Now I wanted to be a part of everything, all at once. Blessedly, our new parish of St. Denis was beginning to offer lifelong education. Adult education was a new concept for me, since Catholics of my time generally thought they learned everything they needed to know in their youth. In important, fundamental ways that is true, but I was ready for more.

One thing I learned was that the church now made a point of placing equal emphasis on the Liturgy of the Word and the Liturgy of the Eucharist. I had always considered the biblical readings to lead to and culminate in the high point of the Eucharist. Was I now to think that hearing God's word at Mass was just as important as receiving the Lord in the sacrament? It was through bible study and in the Mass itself that I began to see that the same Lord who comes to us in his word comes to us in his body.

These lines from Isaiah 55:10-11 made a deep impression on me:

"For just as from the heavens
the rain and snow come down
and do not return there
till they have watered the earth,
making it fertile and fruitful,
giving seed to the one who sows
and bread to the one who eats,
So shall my word be that goes forth from my mouth;
It shall not return to me void,
but shall do my will,
achieving the end for which I sent it."

Two things in this passage from Isaiah stand out. One tells me that I am not on my own, in a state of spiritual infertility, nor are

God's words empty, archaic promises. I have been given all I need to know of his will and assured his will shall reign. From the outset, as a few of us trained to be bible study leaders and were really just learning the basics ourselves, I was encouraged by such a passage that God's revelation of himself is as complete and powerful as we need in order to be his redeemed people.

Another line in Isaiah suggests to me that the sending forth of God's word "from my mouth," as Isaiah describes it, is costly to God. Adam and Eve heard his voice in the garden and turned away in disobedience. Some who listened to Jesus in his lifetime put to death the Word made flesh. Today, his redeemed people still, nevertheless, sin against God.

In my own life, I know that it takes effort to make myself known to others. It is hard for me to reveal myself; and when I succeed, there is still the risk of rejection by others. And so does God bear these risks when he reveals himself to us. But there is a difference. I often count the costs to myself and back away, *but this is not the way God is.*

These kinds of ideas were my preparation for seeing the Liturgy of the Word and the Liturgy of the Eucharist so biblically and sacrificially intertwined that I could think of receiving the Lord in his word and in his body as one. The offering of himself in his word becomes the offering of himself in his human body. And so I began to see that the entire Mass is based on God's revelation of himself in word, and in the deed of the Word made flesh.

We bible students also became mindful that bible study could be a form of prayer, and we began to call ourselves the St. Denis Bible Study/Prayer Group. With only a little effort, I soon found many examples of bible-based prayer and bible-based liturgy in the Mass. I was literally going back and forth between the Mass and the bible every week. Now in the dialogue of the Mass, the people prayed aloud together, but often the prayers or readings dwelt in my mind just long enough, perhaps seconds, extending a thought. I discovered I was praying the bible at Mass.

The great praise song, the *Sanctus*, is a clear example of biblical prayer in every Sunday Mass. We also hear it read in the Gospel on Passion Sunday, when the people greet Jesus on his arrival in

Jerusalem where the Last Supper is soon to take place. The Gospel of John 12:12-16 says:
". . . they took palm branches and went out to meet him, and cried out:
'Hosanna!
Blessed is he who comes in the name of the Lord,
[even] the king of Israel.'"

When we sing the very same Gospel song of praise later in the Mass, everyone—from tired children to the rickety-kneed elderly—rises in anticipation of the arrival of Jesus on our altars and in our midst. The moment brings everyone to life, and we sing together:
"Holy, holy, holy Lord, God of power and might.
Heaven and earth are full of your glory.
Hosanna in the highest.
Blessed is he who comes in the name of the Lord.
Hosanna in the highest."

On the Sunday before Easter people hold branches of palm, which are referred to in the Old Testament as well as in John's Gospel. For many years, I was not aware that parts of the familiar *Sanctus* appear in Psalm 118, a processional hymn for the Jewish Feast of Tabernacles:
"Blessed is he
who comes in the name of the LORD. . . .
Join in procession with leafy branches
up to the horns of the altar."

As I began to read the bible, look up footnotes, and consult commentaries, my biggest surprise was that so many things that are said by or about Jesus in the New Testament come from the Old Testament. Certainly in the case of the *Sanctus* I am moved to think of people, who came before me, saying the same words I say today. It is even more fascinating to think my Christian forbears turned to their Jewish ancestors in faith, using the words of Isaiah, words that came from his heart and that are now so familiar to me.

Since the Mass is primarily a communal form of worship and the people act as one body, in a way we are like the crowd of people from Jerusalem who came out to greet Jesus. The original crowd had been at the nearby town of Bethany, where Jesus had raised Lazarus from the dead and then feasted with him and his sisters. Did the curious gather at the windows and doorway and see Mary, a sister of Lazarus, anoint the feet of Jesus with expensive oil, and did they smell its fragrance when the house became filled with the perfume of the ointment? Did they notice that Jesus was pleased with their anointing and even praised the expense?

Then back in Jerusalem, when the crowd of people who had gone to the feast at nearby Bethany heard that Jesus was coming to Jerusalem, the excitement on the street must have reached a feverish pitch. If Jesus raised a man from the dead in Bethany, what might he do in Jerusalem? Even though the people were of one voice in welcoming Jesus, they were not of one mind that day in Jerusalem. Some had real faith in Jesus, others acted out of hope or curiosity, and still others—we know from the Gospel—plotted against him.

There is a minute or two in the Mass when I always think of that crowd of people. I like to think of them acclaiming Jesus in awesome words and gestures, and to know that through the ages since then other crowds sing out their very words. However, there is uneasiness about this song of praise given to us in both Old and New Testament readings. My thoughts often turn to this: If at Mass I am one of the crowd praising Jesus, singing on the palm-strewn road, am I also part of the crowd which cries out, "Crucify him, crucify him," when Pilate, a few days later, gives the people a chance to free Jesus? Without these Scripture readings and others like them, I would not think this way: I would not think of myself, in my own time, as one among the faithless crowd.

The words of the bible at Mass are not words on a page for me to lift out at will and to pray into being. Surely I pray them, but they have already entered into sacred time and space in the Mass, where they are transformed into something beyond my own will and good intentions. They have their own life now, where word and God meet. They come back to him who formed them, so that speech and speaker are one. His word, as Isaiah says, does not return to him void. It achieves the end for which he sent it.

7

OUR WISDOM

"Whoever boasts, should boast in the Lord."
Epistle, *First Letter of Paul
to the Church at Corinth* 1:31

When our son Joe left home for college and Virg and I drove him out to Ohio, my heart was heavy all 700 miles of the trip. The first day we found his room and met his roommates, but he returned with us for the night to my parents' house. The next day we drove him back to campus for registration and orientation, and that night he had a freshman event to attend. We picked him up that evening, and he again came back to his grandparents' house. The next day, there were more things to do on campus, and he decided to move all his things into his room and spend the night there. I knew the time was fast coming down to our parting.

And so the next morning, we drove over to his dorm to say good-bye—the very break I had been dreading all week. Since I had not said a word to anybody about how I was feeling, hoping to overcome my emotions at the crucial moment, everyone was completely surprised when I totally broke down in sobs. And Joe, who was already at ease in his new environment and looking forward to every minute of it, had a look on his face: What on earth is wrong with Mom?

It was a good thing that I had a new full-time job waiting for me at Dartmouth College. As it happened, I too longed for more study, especially when I had the opportunity, as an employee did, to take courses at the College. After a year, I entered the Master of Arts in Liberal Studies program, taking one course a term.

I began my studies by taking an anthropology course on the beginning of civilizations. My search continued as I took a course in Native American oral literature. A whole other world of belief opened up to me here: One was the "Upward Moving Way of the Navajo" recorded by Father Berard Haile, O.F.M., in 1908. It is a long, structured, fantastic yet reasoned ceremonial that tells how people ascended from prehuman realms to the present world level. Through the ceremonial, healing continues in the present, bringing rebirth, health, and re-creation.

I also came across an Iroquois creation story of the god who is killed and parts of him planted in mounds where, in the Spring, corn emerges as the gift of life for the people. At some length, I studied a Northwest Coast myth of Raven, who creates a world only when he brings light to animals that already are present in an unclassified way in the darkness. Creatures do not really exist until, with the light, Raven sees and names each kind of creature.

At this point I knew quite a few myths but had no foundation to analyze or understand them. I then took a course on myth, ritual, and symbolism that covered several methodologies in use for the academic study of these topics. The methodologies came out of psychology, sociology, and modern linguistics. I was not accustomed to a study of the elements of religion other than that offered by theology itself.

Although I was very interested in these studies—religion is to some extent a construct of human thought—I decided over time that in themselves these studies did not lead to an overall explanation of the interactions of God and man. Essentially, they did not consider the idea that myth and ritual can be true aspects of divine revelation, for the humanities only examine the human side of things. I admired some of the myths I had studied for a theological quality even more than any humanistic quality I found in them. I came to appreciate theology—especially my own Catholic theology—more than ever. A study of God must at least consider the methods God uses to reveal himself.

Sometimes the corn myth surprisingly came to mind when I was at Mass. The idea of the one who is sacrificed to provide life for others has something in common with the sacrifice of Christ for our redemption: The perfect, divine one is the lone savior of his people. I also began to concentrate more on the materiality of the Eucharist, the physical presence of consecrated, life-giving bread. In the Eucharist, God acts within my body first in a physical way as food. God nourishes my body with his own, in the form of bread, in effect recreating me with himself. Creation of the body and redemption of the soul become intimately bound to each other: They both give life.

But if myths and rituals of the sacrificed god exist throughout human history, what is different about Jesus Christ? He alone, I think, is the promised Son of God who comes to man in time, in response to an ages-long awaiting and a promise to make right what was lost in their relationship all the way back to the beginning of human experience. Furthermore, Christ brought all that he is to everyone who is, in ways far beyond the expectations of men of clans and tribes, in making known the one God of all—his Father. Finally, his is a willing self-sacrifice of love.

In one of my courses I learned that the word "religion" comes from the Latin "religio" and means, "to link." In any religion people are linked together in their beliefs and experiences of God. In some ways, people of all religions are also linked to each other. In my Christian belief, I see this phenomenon as an example of the ongoing work of the Holy Spirit—one who patiently moves people in their souls from where they are, to follow Jesus Christ to God the Father— the Giver of Life.

I had an opportunity to learn something about another of the world's religions during a year off my studies, when Virg and I went to Japan, China, and Korea for a few weeks. During our stay in Japan I observed the practice of the Shinto religion in several places, with information offered by a good friend who is Korean. He told us that Shinto has no temple and very little ritual. Rather it has shrines to the dead and worships its ancestors. At the important Meiji Shrine in Tokyo, I saw people throw out their arms and clap once, then clap twice more and bow. There were boxes for throwing in coins and a wishing board where people hang small wooden signs with petitions on them. Another day I visited the Great Buddha and Shinto shrines in Kamakura that date to the twelfth century. My friend was right:

There was very little ritual and Shinto seemed about as different as another major religion could be from my own.

Of course, I had been mostly to tourist sites, and so one day, back in Tokyo, I set out on my own, following a map that had a symbol for shrines. With the help of a policeman, I found myself on Yakauni-dori, a very wide street in a business district, in search of a shrine called Hanazono Jinja. I found it between two office buildings, its long entryway marked by a Shinto arch. A narrow walk led behind the buildings to a courtyard. There I passed a cleansing well where people wash their hands before approaching the shrine.

It was late morning and a steady stream of people, young and old, were coming and going quickly, clapping and bowing, and leaving their offerings and petitions. The actions were the same as at other shrines, but here ordinary people were stopping by in the midst of their busy day for a prayer—probably a petition.

Life is what ancestors give us, as well as the means and culture within which to live it. They give us our names and our identities. And they give us our spiritual heritage and continuing guidance. I admire the Japanese for honoring their ancestors, and I suspect that their reverence of ancestors in the Shinto religion is linked to belief in the Giver of Life.

Later in the week, I met three young women at dinner and asked them what Japanese people believe. One said that all Japanese believe in some god. Shintoism believes that God creates all things and that spirits exist in all things, they explained. Shintoism is for this life, for good crops, good health and the like, while Buddhism provides the moral behavior and after-life. They agreed that the same people practice the two religions—and in their opinion, people do not take very seriously the visiting of shrines and temples, which I had witnessed only as a stranger. On the latter point, I privately disagreed, remembering those ordinary people I had seen at the shrine.

By the time Joe was a sophomore, our daughter Sheila started as a freshman at a college in upstate New York. I knew that Sheila was more apprehensive about leaving home and beginning a new stage in her life than Joe had been. But the tables were turned on me the morning we went by her dorm to say good-bye. I was being brave this time around and so was caught by surprise when I saw her there, standing on the edge of the curb in front of her dorm, so young with her beautiful hair in curls all over her head, waiting for us. Her big blue eyes filled with teardrops that rolled down her face, and, as always happened when she cried, I had the feeling of wanting to reach out and wipe away her tears. We hugged and reassured her that we would be back soon for Parents' Weekend. That weekend seemed a long time away.

I did not know then, with Sheila or with Joe, that this was the beginning of my life without my children. I still expected that they were going away for a little while which would be good for them and for us. They would come back to reclaim their bedrooms and their own chairs at the table, even the wooden napkin holders on which someone had burned their names. Of course they came home for holidays and to spend the summers, although Joe only the first summer. It seems my tears had actually been prophetic, as Joe from that time has always lived far from us. There were no parting tears two years later when Brenda started at Dartmouth. She had been attracted to our hometown college in part because of Aquinas House, the Catholic student center, which she had begun to attend while still in high school. Brenda would be close by, and she and I could almost compare notes!

The truth of the matter is that college is a time to experience the ideas of other people—professors and other scholars, and also new friends and roommates from other backgrounds. I was all in favor of that, but a little rebuffed when the experience of faith and family, which had been the center of their lives, seemed to take second place. Sheila studied in France her entire third year in college and when she came home I felt that we were all not *French* enough to suit her! About that time, Brenda joined a bible study group in which she heard untrue things about the Catholic Church, and she believed *them!*

Eventually, my Master's thesis turned out to be an assessment of Joseph Campbell, the professor turned celebrity guru, who at the time was popularizing mythology on television. Earlier he was known for his four volumes of *The Masks of God*, on which I based my study. Wrestling with my subject, one that had undergone very little critical review, I recognized that Campbell knew a great deal about the myths of the world but that his attempts to define a theory of mythology failed. I thought the fault was due to his insistence that the individual is the hero of his own mythology; and to his idea that modern man has internalized sacrifice and so has no need of saving or being saved. His password to his audiences was a pretty limp example of moral advice: "Follow your bliss."

In the first case, Campbell actually denuded mythology of what it is—the *sharing* of structured supernatural beliefs in narrative form. And in terms of sacrifice, it seemed to me that if his modern man does not in fact act to save another, he is not really a hero—even in his own eyes; nor is he likely to admit his own need for the saving help of another.

While I studied for six years, all three children completed their own four years in turn at their colleges. I shared some of their experience by studying myself during their college years, but I had more knowledge of life. I knew what I believed. I also had experience of suffering and loss. It matters whether the giving of the self is actual and dedicated and not only philosophical or symbolic. I believed in God the Father who is the Giver of Life and in God the Son who gives up his life for others. And when I remembered him, I believed in God the Holy Spirit whose essence has always been wisdom.

As St. Paul tells me in his letter, God has made me a member of Christ Jesus, and he has become my wisdom for which I do not boast.

8

GO TELL EVERYONE

"The homily is a prophetic moment in the liturgy, and the
homilist like a prophet sees deeply into reality, presents the
Gospel vision, heals our blindness and calls us to fidelity."

Go Tell Everyone
Rev. James McKarns

At every Mass I think of my children. I think of being with them
when they were young, and I think of them now, being with
their own young families. Parents want to do all the right things for
their children, and they hope that when they bring their children up
in the church, they will be educated, strengthened, and grace-filled
for their entire lives. Such parents choose the right goal, but children
have many bumps along the way, just as their parents did. How I pray
for my children and their children, that they always draw closer to
God. The Mass is the fundamental Catholic way to express faith on
the one hand and to build it up on the other.

There was a tendency among Catholics of my time, who had gone
to Catholic schools themselves, to think that taking our children to
Mass and religious instruction was the better part of our job. I
thought my appreciation for the Mass and for being Catholic was
going to just rub off on my children. I was quiet about how much
it meant to me. I could have done a much better job of telling them
how wondrous I thought the Mass was, not just that we all were
going together! Families do many wonderful things together, but
they are not all "wondrous."

Our son Joe wanted to drop out of religious education in his junior
year of high school, and I saw this as an either/or situation: Either
he wanted to go, or we forced him. I didn't think of a reasonable

middle way such as encouraging him by helping to strengthen his faith. This could have been a listening and teaching time on my part, but it was not, to my later dismay. As a college student living far away, he stopped going to Mass. A few years later when he met Vickie and they wanted to get married, he was not known at any church. He inquired at a Catholic church and was told he would have to wait the standard six months and complete the marriage preparation course.

He and Vickie wanted to get married sooner than that, and so I attended my son's wedding before a justice of the peace in a park in Massillon, Ohio. Misgivings were put aside by the seriousness and joy of the bride and groom and by the beauty of their vows, as well as by the good words of the justice of the peace. The couple had put together this ceremony for themselves, and later we had a sort of potluck supper with friends and relatives contributing to the wedding feast.

Later, when I saw the wedding photos, I could detect a trace of sadness in my own face. From my vantage point, I had seen a door close on my son and his bride, a door at a church where they had knocked but it had not opened for them. A nuptial Mass would have been more than icing on the cake! A nuptial Mass is dedicated to the wedding couple, the sacrifice of Christ is offered for them, and they receive sacramental grace for their married life. These are powerful graces, and I wondered: Would they ever knock on a church door again?

When our first grandchild, Clay Joseph, was born, and Joe and Vickie were still unaffiliated with a church, I asked Joe if he wanted to have Clay baptized. He said he did. I wasn't sure if we were both talking about Baptism as a Catholic. Vickie was raised a Protestant, so I didn't know what she thought about this. I suggested to Joe that if he and Vickie agreed about a Catholic Baptism, they should seek out and talk to the priest at the nearest Catholic church in the new town where they had just moved. This would truly be a new beginning. I was sure they could figure this out for themselves, but I had to say something!

For two months, nothing happened. I didn't press the subject, for after all Clay was their child and it was their decision. I also was eager to see what they did about this on their own, since I believe that parents do their adult children no favor by arranging things like weddings and Baptisms for them through their own channels.

One of the happiest moments of my life came as a surprise the day Joe called to say, "Mom, I just wanted to tell you that Clay is being baptized at St. Barbara's Church tomorrow." He sounded absolutely joyful. And then, as if my cup were not overflowing, he added, "and Vickie and I will soon be starting RCIA [Rite of Christian Initiation for Adults]."

How had all this come about? Joe, Vickie, and Clay had met Father James McKarns! It was Vickie who called St. Barbara's parish and talked to the pastor about Baptism. He told her that if they came to Mass at St. Barbara's the next three Sundays he would then baptize Clay on the third Sunday. They would show their sincerity in this reasonably small way—and I presume the three weeks gave Father McKarns a chance to get to know them better. He also suggested RCIA, which was just beginning that fall, for both Joe and Vickie, who I later learned had first wanted to become a Catholic when she was a teenager.

The new family of three went off to RCIA every week for the next six months. From all reports, the young parents got a lot from it and met people who helped them along this path. It seemed to me that every young family could benefit from something like RCIA. One parishioner even came to the house occasionally to stay with Clay for a couple hours while Vickie had some time away by herself. On Easter Sunday, Vickie came into the church, and on another occasion, she and Joe repeated their marriage vows in the church.

My husband and I got to know this parish and Father McKarns during our visits and liked going to St. Barbara's for Mass. Not only were we reunited in this way with our family, but also we benefited from Father McKarns's wonderful, short, poignant homilies that contained real lessons. I am indebted to all the priests in my life who have preached wonderful homilies, but some are truly exceptional. Father McKarns was one of them.

After Mass one day, at our bidding, he showed us his published books: *Go Tell Everyone,* a commentary on the Sunday readings at Mass for the A, B, and C yearly cycles, which I brought home; and a three-volume set of daily meditations for the cycles, titled *Give Us*

This Day, which Joe got. These three-year cycles focus on the Gospels of Matthew, Mark, and Luke in turn.

With his gift for preaching, Father McKarns wrote the books as an aid for other homilists and also for lay persons who are readers at Mass or who desire to follow the Liturgy of the Word more fully. He and his books are examples of the revitalization of the Scripture-based homily in the church following Vatican II.

Clay's little brother, Scott Joseph, was born two and a half years later, and we were able to make the trip for his Baptism by Father McKarns. I wrote in my journal about the Mass and the Baptism, when we his family—speaking for Scott and for ourselves—renounced Satan and all his works. The Gospel of the Mass was right in tune with Scott's Baptism that followed it, since this happened to be the first Sunday of Lent in Cycle A. The Gospel was fittingly Matthew 4:1-11, on the temptation of Christ by Satan in the wilderness:

"Father McKarns preached on the temptations presented to the mind of Jesus—bread , glory, and possessions. This reading and sermon seemed appropriate for a day of Baptism. Baptism reminds us that the life of a child of God needs to be strong. Another reading from Genesis 2 and 3 showed how God breathed life into Adam but then Adam, exercising his free will, quickly lost his supernatural life by turning away from God.

"Father McKarns anointed Scott with the chrism of salvation, and his father, Joe, lighted a candle from the paschal candle. This candle was then given to Joe for Scott with a reminder to light it each year on the anniversary of his Baptism, the true beginning of his life.

"I marvel at God's ways. Here are Joe, Vickie, Clay, and now Scott, a family newly committed to their lives in Christ. Vickie has told me many times that she always wanted to be a Catholic. During this visit, she told me she had many friends who were Catholic when she was growing up and that she had once attended an ordination. It was the most

beautiful thing she ever saw. Her mother would not let her
become a Catholic at that time (rightly so, I thought)."

Not long after Scott's Baptism, Father McKarns received a new
assignment from his bishop. We would miss him on our visits, but
he had been in the right place at the right time for our son and his
family, and I will always be grateful to him. He could have closed
the door on a stranger.

Two years later, our whole family traveled to Minnesota for
the wedding of Sheila and Tom. Sheila was then a school librarian
in Minneapolis. Tom's uncle, Father John Brandes, came home to
Minnesota from his mission in Guatemala to marry them, and he
was almost as resplendent in his floor-length stole of many colors as
the bride in her white satin gown.

Father Brandes read the Gospel of John 2:1-12 that is a favorite
at Catholic weddings. It is the story of Christ's first miracle when he
changes water into wine and this new wine is the best wine. Christ's
presence at the wedding has always had meaning for Catholics
with its mark of divine approval on marriage—as well as its strong
intimations for new wine, as it is Jesus himself who is the "new wine"
of the gospels.

In his homily, Father Brandes also talked about another miracle:
"For Tom and Sheila, their marriage is a miracle of their love and
well-practiced faith being brought together." I thought back to the
years when Sheila, at one point in her mid-twenties, had made
a decision to be a more serious and observant Catholic than she
thought she had been. In her own generation, first at college and then
in the work community, she did not have much support for growth
as a young adult Catholic.

As a result of that, and because she needed a teaching job, Sheila
decided to take a position in San Antonio, Texas, teaching for two
years at a Catholic school as a volunteer for VESS (Volunteers for
Educational and Social Services) in that diocese. There she met some
young Catholics from Minnesota and through them she later met
Tom. He was no nominal, cultural, 'brought-up-a-Catholic,' but a
mature man of prayer and charity. Yes, I could see, each one brings
love and well-practiced faith to the other in this marriage.

Father Brandes went on to say: "We're standing here on the shoulders of the generations who have borne children. Sheila's grandparents. They're here. Tom's grandparents. They're here. Now, this is the miracle of the Lunardini and Brandes families [of the fathers of the bride and groom] and the Murphy and Herrigas families [of the mothers of the bride and groom]. This is the first time they have come together. It's their miracle today."

Marriage is familial and ancestral not only for the husband and wife but each one's family becomes a part of their lives together. And then in the miracle of their children, both ancestral lines converge. I admit to thinking of family generations as passing on religion as well as genes. Sheila's grandparents were now both dead, as were Tom's, and Tom's father. They were present in my heart and prayers of thanksgiving at this wedding Mass.

And then after the homily, before entering into the great sacramental mystery of the Mass, Tom and Sheila came forward to say their vows as husband and wife. The wedding was wonderful, certainly in our own tradition. But I am always overcome by a sense of sadness that we all are not truly one. Weddings bring two families together, but not all members of either family continue to fully share a faith they once had so much in common that it was as simple as breathing. I think it can actually be sad or troubling at these times for everyone, perhaps especially for those who are on the "outside" for any reason. Some are not as much at home here as others. They may have left the church, as our daughter Brenda; they may be divorced and remarried, as a few relatives of both families; or for their own reasons, they may simply not be close to the church.

Closest to me of those who have left the Catholic faith is my daughter Brenda, who in college became an evangelical Protestant. She married Luke, a serious, lifelong Protestant at Valley Bible Church, and they brought their four-month-old son Phineas to Sheila and Tom's wedding. Brenda's decision, which I lament in part because it means loss of the Mass and Holy Communion for her, reminds me that she and I have Protestant forbears as well as the Catholic ones. At times I can see the Methodist grandfather I never knew, reading his bible and preparing his sermons in the evening after his day's work was done. Or I see my grandmother washing dishes at the back-porch pump, singing some beloved hymn as my mother did at our kitchen sink in later years. I am overwhelmed at times by the strong Christian faith of these people, my grandparents on my mother's side, and the faith which I now see in Brenda's family. The faith of my grandparents is something I know about but did not personally witness; in Brenda, it is something I can truly see for myself.

On special occasions such as weddings, priests sometimes make a judgment to invite all baptized Christians to receive Holy Communion. After his homily, Father Brandes did so. Referring to Jesus who becomes the new wine—the best wine—of the Gospel, he said: "In this Eucharist we have the new wine presented to us and we invite all the baptized to participate."

Such an invitation keeps open the door so that anyone can enter. Father Brandes didn't just marry two people that day. He was also a homilist who saw the reality of the day, saw those on the outside, and presented the Gospel vision—one of an invitation that goes back to Jesus Christ.

9

CREDO

"We believe in one God, the Father, the Almighty . . .
We believe in one Lord, Jesus Christ, the only Son of God . . .
We believe in the Holy Spirit, the Lord, the giver of life . . ."
Profession of Faith
Saint Andrew Bible Missal, 1982

The "I believe" of the Latin *Credo* changed to "we believe" when the people began to pray the Nicene Creed aloud together in English at Mass. I suppose the reason was that in the *Novus Ordo* Mass which features dialogue, "we" makes more sense than "I"; however, if everyone were to say "I believe," the result is still a collective prayer.

The *Credo* is a different kind of prayer in that it does not directly address God: It does not praise him, nor thank him, nor ask for forgiveness or blessing from him. It can appear as a series of very short statements that fly out of our mouths as if we were engaged in a test, one that we pass if we say all of the words quickly and correctly.

However, it is truly a prayer, not a test. More than any other Mass prayer, it speaks of the three persons in one God and what each one of them *does.* It is well placed after we have just heard the word of God proclaimed and explained. Now as the first part of the Mass, the Liturgy of the Word, comes to an end, the time is right for us to stand up and say, "we believe."

The best way I have found to say our profession of faith, the Nicene Creed, is to put aside questions about it within the Mass itself. Examination of any of the statements of belief within the Creed best takes place in times outside of Mass. In the last twenty-five years, reading reliable and orthodox sources of knowledge and inspiration gradually helped mature the faith of my childhood on which I coasted for some years. Some of my best sources are the bible (usually the *Reader's Edition of the Jerusalem Bible*) and biblical commentaries; spiritual writers such as Henri Nouwen, Adrienne von Speyr, and Mother Teresa; theologians from Scott Hahn to Cardinal Schonborn to John Paul II; certain encyclicals and apostolic letters of recent times; and the *Catechism of the Catholic Church*.

Adrienne von Speyr's meditations on Elijah and the Gospel of John have led me into a new way—first, of reading the bible; then of praying the Mass. While her books are profound biblical studies, even better, they are profound biblical meditations. I gain from them some idea of a method of contemplative reading. This same prayerful reading, concentrating on the words of the bible, can be transferred to hearing, reading, and speaking the words of the Mass—and this has become my way of being present at Mass.

It seems that I can go just so far with study of the things of God. Study is so important—I *want* to know and understand—but if I wrestle on and on, demanding to know and understand more than is forthcoming from an honest effort, then I am out of touch with my proper limits in regard to the majesty of God. The grace and divine life he gives me—the spark that illuminates him—are still and always dependent on him. If I give up the struggle of always having questions and objections, there comes an openness that is filled by one thing: faith. And that is all the Creed asks of me. It does not require that I understand.

Now I find the Creed to be not so much a series of dogmatic statements as a litany. Its words sing in my heart for a moment before they are released in my voice. In its own way, the *Credo* is a *Gloria!*

Even so, I allow a struggle with the concepts of the Creed to persist to some extent in times outside of Mass when, for example, my husband asks: What does it mean to say Jesus Christ is the Son of God, eternally begotten of the Father? He and I discuss this subject from time to time, sitting in our easy chairs back home after Mass. Virg thinks that Arius made some strong points at the Council of Nicea, and I, of course, follow Athanasius who won the day.

Arius took the title "Son of God" to mean that Jesus is secondary to the Father. In his view, the Father is superior to and has primacy over the Son. Athanasius' breakthrough was to see God as giving all of himself in begetting the Son. In this way I can see the naming of the "Son" by the Father and the calling of God "Father" by the Son as an ongoing relationship of closeness between the two. It is, I can only imagine, a part of their secret life in each other with the immense joy of the giver and the eternal surprise of the receiver, returning love for love in fullness so that there is no distinction of measure between giver and receiver. This is just one way Jesus is the image of the Father, a perfect image, a perfect Son. This is so because he bears in himself the divinity, creativity, eternity, authority, and will of the Father, so that he is all that the Father is.

Some of this opened up to me when I read Cardinal Christoph Schonborn's *God's Human Face*. First, to see how the Son is coequal with his Father. Then, with the Son and the Father one, to see how each is still a distinct person. The Father, who has the quality of always-being in himself, creates a Son, distinct from himself; and the Father gives his own always-beingness to his Son in his own person. Even more to consider is the all-lovingness of the Father, who gives the Son his all-lovingness. Only love gives love; and only love can give all of one's identity.

I certainly always believed in the love of the Father, yet for a long time upheld more his other divine powers such as eternity, creativity, authority—perhaps unwittingly reserving love as a special attribute of the Son. By grace, I began to see the Father's love as the center from which radiates the rest of his beingness.

Athanasius' way of looking at the relationship of the Father and Son clears the way for understanding all that is revealed about the Son in the bible. In Arius's theology, the Son would be essentially only a demigod, unworthy to fulfill the Father's plan of salvation. The Holy Spirit, who is one with the Father and Son and who makes fruitful the one divine will in the world, seems to have been at work in the world at the Council of Nicea in 325 A.D. There the Church decided that Athanasius had the best understanding of the concepts of Father and Son as they are revealed in the bible. And it is this Council's creed, the Nicene Creed, which is our *Credo*.

In recent years, I discovered the French poet Paul Claudel who wrote about the victorious struggle that is contained in the *Credo*:

"When in my village church I hear the *Credo* being recited, one article after another . . . I tremble with inner ecstasy; it seems to me that I am present at the creation of the world. I know the cost of each one of those formulae printed in eternal truth—with what rending of heaven and earth, what rivers of blood, by what effort, what mental travail, and with what overflowing grace they came to be born. I see those great masses of dogma emerge and take form before my eyes one after the other; I see man struggling painfully and finally succeeding in tearing out of his own heart, the final affirmation." (*Epee*, 64, quoted in *I Believe in God*).

The most awesome lines in the *Credo* are at the beginning:
"We believe in one God,
the Father Almighty,
maker of heaven and earth,
of all that is seen and unseen."

Looking at the first line of the *Credo*, I am reminded of the year that my church's Evening Bible Study Group used the video study series "Our Father's Plan" by Scott Hahn and Jeff Cavins as a guide to the historical books of the bible. More people came that year than ever before, probably because both men are well-known for their books and appearances on the Eternal Word Television Network. For Hahn, the Fatherhood of God is what is revealed in the bible: God is the eternal Father of the Son, and he is our Father through his mercy and grace. This family model is not a metaphor we use for God; it is the way God is, and the way he models family for us.

I also remember Hahn's commentary on Genesis 2:2: "Since on the seventh day God was finished with the work he had been doing, he rested on the seventh day. . . ." In his work of creation, God leaves us with a pattern for our own rest. He gives us a goal that appears to have been his own goal for creation: a day beyond the days of work, a day on which he sees that everything he made is good. The seventh day is the day for which we are truly created. It seems to me that we may call that day "heaven," a resting in divinity.

Looking ahead in the Creed, we say this about the Son:
"For us men and for our salvation
he came down from heaven."

Here there is an interruption in the life of the beloved Son, resting in the Father's rest. He comes into a hostile world, fallen out of the grace with which God created human life. The bible tells us that the cause of the fall is willful disobedience to divine will. God gives his law—born of who he is to his people with the foreknowledge of their failure. And still he gives, and gives, and gives through covenants, patriarchs, prophets and kings, until only One is left, the "eternally begotten of the Father." This One who rests in his Father's arms in eternity consents to come. He wills what the Father wills:
"by the power of the Holy Spirit
he was born of the Virgin Mary and became man."

We know what follows, as we say:
"For our sake he was crucified under Pontius Pilate;
he suffered, died, and was buried."

For our sake, the Son—in becoming man and living the Father's law of love in the world—suffers the cost. And so does the Trinity of three persons in one God who in their unity bring forth the presence of the Son in the world. Through the actions of the Trinity, Claudel's "one article after another . . . those formulae printed in eternal truth" bear witness to the struggle and victory of our redemption.

Following the Son, others come to bear the fruits of salvation to all the people of the world, to write down the gospels and epistles, to teach and to preach, and to build up, in the words of the *Credo*:
" . . . one holy catholic and apostolic Church."

The *Credo* lives on, calling Claudel's man to finally succeed "in tearing out of his own heart the final affirmation." For an article of the *Credo* is lost if it does not find a heart which accepts it. As a Catholic, I like to say that faith is a gift of God, but the phrase does not convey the struggle in coming to that "final affirmation"—not of a vague god of my own making but of one who reveals himself to me. There must have been a point in my life, unknown to me now, at which I threw overboard anything that stood in the way of saying, "I believe in God." I think that in my life I choose to accept the gift, choose to believe. I do not know any other way to put it. I want the gift. I want to believe. And like the father whose son is possessed by a mute spirit in the Gospel of Mark 9:24, I also need to say, "I do believe, help my unbelief."

At the very end of the *Credo* is this:
"We look for the resurrection of the dead,
and the life of the world to come. Amen."

At Mass on Sunday, it seems to me that as I look to the life of the world to come, the divine life of the world comes to me, greets me, and rests with me awhile.

10
HUMAN HANDS

"Blessed are you, Lord, God of all creation.
Through your goodness we have this bread to offer,
which earth has given and human hands have made.
It will become for us the bread of life."

Preparation of the gifts
Saint Andrew Bible Missal, 1982

In the second part of the Mass, the liturgy of the Eucharist begins with the priest preparing the altar, then taking in his hands the gifts—first the bread and blessing it, and then the cup of wine, with similar words:

"Blessed are you, Lord, God of all creation
Through your goodness we have this wine to offer,
fruit of the vine and work of human hands.
It will become our spiritual drink."

The wheat and grapes of which the bread and wine are made were planted and tended by human hands according to the plan of the God of all creation. Then our God who is all beauty inspires his people to take these fruits and further produce of them these two most artful forms of food—bread and wine.

People who grow food know the hard work of it, but what a wondrous thing to be assured that this food has been chosen by God himself, not only to sustain our lives but to be acceptable to him as tangible, material offerings in his memorial sacrifice. Jesus might have skipped the Last Supper of his life, leaving us with his teachings and blessings and promises of eternal life. That would have been wonder enough, but there was more. Through his goodness he blessed into eternity this "work of human hands," taking it, making it holy, and giving it back to us consecrated into his body and blood. This is not a supper anymore; it is a sacrifice. It is a sacrifice because Jesus did it willingly, with love, for a transcendent reason, and at great cost to himself.

In the Old Testament, first the heads of families and later the priests offered unblemished cows, goats, and sheep on their altars. These animals, also gifts of creation and signs of human work, were slaughtered and wholly burned; and the blood—sign of the animals' life and vitality—was offered separately in these sacrifices performed at times of purification, consecration, and celebration.

Other offerings were partly burned as either peace or atonement sacrifices. In peace offerings, the fat was offered on the altar and the rest of the animal was consumed in a banquet. Atonement sacrifices were offered to restore God's favor when people had offended him unwittingly through their faults or because they had been in contact with some unclean thing. There was no sacrifice in which people atoned for their willful sins. Forgiveness for sin was obtained only by repentance, a point made by biblical scholar John McKenzie, S.J., whose work I have consulted for many years.

There were intimations of a new sacrifice, for example, in Isaiah 53:11:

"Through his suffering, my servant shall justify many,
and their guilt he shall bear."

These are signs of an astounding change that would be fulfilled by Jesus, who would become both high priest and victim. One who would willingly offer as priest, his own life as victim, even on behalf of the knowing, willing, yet unrepentant, sinner.

In the Gospel of John 6:51, as Passover and his own passion and death approach, Jesus tells the people:

"I am the living bread that came down from heaven;
whoever eats this bread will live forever; and the bread that I
will give is my flesh for the life of the world."

When I hear these words, I think back to Genesis and the story of how death came into the world through the first human sin of disobedience. This was the sin shared by humankind who would also share in its forgiveness, for Jesus reached into the abyss and lifted us out of it. In his self-sacrificing obedience, he redeemed one and all.

At Mass I think of my own part in God's work on earth, so that I can offer it along with the redemptive work of Jesus, to the Father. Do I perform my work willingly, with love, for God's purpose, and at cost to myself? Whatever I am and do in this way constitutes my own offering. Most of the time, the work of my own human hands has something to do with food, just as it had for my Mother!

When I was growing up, we all waited to eat until after Mass, a required fast from midnight on, often making our first meal of the day on Sunday sometime around noon. But then what a breakfast we had! Grapefruit, eggs and bacon, and toast or coffee cake. When I was in elementary school, we went from home directly to Mass on the first Friday of each month, again fasting until after we had been to Holy Communion. What a wonderful aroma then greeted us as we lined up in the school cafeteria, where some of our mothers had prepared cauldrons of steaming hot chocolate, served with the greatest sugary donuts I ever tasted. What a great way it was to start a school day.

At home on Sundays, soon after our late breakfast, my mother began to prepare dinner which usually involved putting on a pot roast and later adding potatoes, carrots, and onions. It would cook all afternoon by itself, while she made one of her fabulous pies—lemon, chocolate or butterscotch meringue; or apple, peach, or cherry, depending on the season. On special occasions like birthdays and Easter, there was a snowy-white, fresh-coconut cake. Mother often took dinner and the sixth piece of a pie or part of a cake to some elderly person she knew. Sunday afternoons were also a time to visit or be visited, usually unannounced! It was supposed to be even more of a pleasure if good friends surprised each other by dropping by.

My father had a small vegetable garden in Ohio in the 1960s, 70s, and 80s, just as his father had in Indiana in the 1920s, 30s, and 40s. I still have my father's and grandfather's garden basket, which I have used for many years to gather produce from our own twenty by fifty-foot garden in Hanover. Almost everywhere we have lived, my husband and I have had a garden. For me, helping him grow food is just the beginning, since it must all in due time be gathered, cleaned, and prepared for the table. This is one thing that is the work of our human hands, as it is for all of the earth's peoples.

As I read old letters from my parents I notice how so many of their activities and concerns were centered close to home. My father was more interested in world affairs than my mother, but so much of the attention of both of them was given to everyday matters. My parents were primarily interested in their family, friends, and neighbors, and Mother was often the one to see that love and friendship got translated into action. She was good to visit people who were sick or lonely and frequently reminded my Father of his responsibility to aging relatives. She tried to lift people's spirits and did not shrink from those who were close to death. Both my parents comforted friends who were in mourning, and, probably because of their own experience in losing one of their children, they had a bond with others who went through this particular grief.

This way of offering themselves was part of my parents' example to me, so that I naturally tend to want to be like them; yet in some ways I will never be like them. I'm figuring it out as I go along, so that whatever my way of offering myself in life may be, it is my gift to present at the altar.

During the preparation of the gifts at Mass, I see that anything I am and do that is good is my offering. Once I heard of a musician who died, and at his funeral Mass his friends placed his musical instrument at the foot of the altar. I could not help but wonder if there was anything that might be placed there at the end of *my* life. What would I want to be placed there? What have *my* hands produced? I began to imagine a sampling of children's stories and newspaper and magazine articles that came from my hands as well as my mind. I quickly gave up this idea as being, for one thing, too prideful. God alone knows the truest gift I bring, and it is impossible to know what God knows about me.

My mother's work came to an end when she was diagnosed with ovarian cancer. From then on, in the depths of incurable suffering, she began her retreat from the world. Her work in life—being a daughter, sister, wife, mother, grandmother, and friend—done with so much love that it often caused her pain, was found worthy, I believe, by the Father. Despite bouts of depression she did her part, lent her hands to the work of the Lord all her life. At her funeral Mass, when the priest went to the door of the church to bless and escort her body to the altar, I heard him pray:

"When Bonnie was baptized, she put on Christ. Let her now be clothed in glory."

My father lived for another twelve years, always young at heart, making new friends, and taking on new challenges. In his eighties, he went to the men's prison on Sunday evenings and played pool and other games with the inmates. He sometimes got into trouble because of his quick temper, but people had to like the other side of him—the smiling eyes as his humor broke through. For 40 years, he had been a member of the St. Vincent dePaul Society and continued as president of his parish chapter when he was 80. Beginning in the 1950s, the eight members of the group met each Friday morning after early Mass. When prayer and business were over, I learned many years later, a secret collection was taken. When I was growing up, my father would sometimes get a call after work "about St. Vincent dePaul" and be on his way that evening. He never told us what the group did, or for whom, although I thought it involved providing emergency funds from the Society for people in financial straits. Helping our own parish families turned out to be just one part of their work.

Suffering from glaucoma, my father had some near misses with driving. When finally he began to cut back, he did so one destination at a time. The last one to go was driving to daily Mass. His driving there even made the priest nervous. But my father had always been sure that he could get to Mass and back safely, that surely God—or Johnny—was watching over him. In desperation to keep him off the road, his friend Marty, also a Notre Dame man, began to pick him up for daily Mass and then bring him back to his retirement village apartment. On my last visit to Ohio, he no longer had the car. I had wrenched it from him by giving my son $500 to buy it, keeping his beloved Olds in the family for awhile longer. And so my father and I went to Mass on Sunday together on the shuttle bus. He was so pleased with having this backup transportation that I wondered why he had resisted it for so long.

Then he who had carried me to church as an infant and watched over all of us could no longer see well enough to follow me back to our seats after Holy Communion. Little strokes took out memory, and then one day he suffered the stroke that took his life, like his father and grandfather before him.

When my sister and I met with the priest to plan my father's funeral Mass, we asked if the organist could play the Notre Dame Victory March as we left the church. We knew of no other piece of music he loved as much and thought that it would be proper enough. The words sing of human striving through Our Lady, *Notre Dame:*

> "Cheer, cheer for old Notre Dame,
> Wake up the echoes cheering her name,
> Send a volley cheer on high,
> Shake down the thunder from the sky.
> What though the odds be great or small
> Old Notre Dame will win over all,
> While her loyal sons are marching,
> Onward to victory."

The priest was agreeable to this suggestion but not sure if the music was at hand. On the morning of the funeral as we began to walk out of my father's church with him for the last time, hoping to hear the Notre Dame song, the organ began to play "When Irish Eyes are Smiling." It was a surprise, but it was just right. Although the words were not sung, they didn't have to be; they were imprinted upon us long ago:

> "When Irish eyes are smiling
> for it's like a morn in Spring.
> In the lilt of Irish laughter
> you can hear the angels sing."

Faith. Hope. Love. Memory. Loyalty. Friendship. Effort. Sacrifice. These were my parents' ways of being themselves. These were the ways they did their work in life, and these were their offering of themselves to God.

In the Mass, I unite the gift of myself to the gifts of others, to the great gift of Christ himself, to the Father. Imperfect gifts bound to the perfect gift. This can be so only because Christ asks us to join him at Supper. It is as if, once gathered there, he tells us, his brothers and sisters: *I have found the perfect gift for Our Father. Let it be from all of us. Let us all contribute to the gift. Let it be from all of us.*

11

FATHER AND SON

"Father, all powerful and ever-living God
We do well always and everywhere to give you thanks
through Jesus Christ our Lord."

Preface of Lent I
Magnificat, 2006

The Preface is a good example of Christian prayer and so familiar that it is easy to overlook the impact of its meaning: a prayer of praise and thanks to the Father—*through* Christ our Lord. Prayer is always offered to the Father who is "all powerful" and "ever-living," because that is the way of Christ who follows the Father's will and brings all to him.

Christ is and always has been the Son, begotten of the Father in eternity so that what exists is the timeless love of the Father for the Son and of the Son for the Father. The Son is his own person, but he has all the attributes of his Father and so he is "all powerful" and "ever-living." These are divine attributes of the Father given to the Son. Since the Father is not limited in any way—he is God—he can give all of himself.

Then the Father sends his Son into the world that observes the passing of time. His human birth marks the beginning of our redemption, in which he brings back his children to the Father. All that I know of the Father I know through the words of the Son, and the Son says: "Whoever has seen me has seen the Father. . . . I am in the Father and the Father is in me. . . . And whoever loves me will be loved by my Father." (John 14:9; 11; and 21.)

All people are to give thanks to the Father, because that is what the Son models for us. Gratitude is the spirit in which to pray the

Preface. Here it is that the entire world which the Father created is placed at his feet with gratitude by the Son in the Mass. And hailing the Son, who asks no glory for himself, the Preface concludes with the singing of the *Sanctus:*

> ". . . Blessed is he who comes in the name of the Lord.
> Hosanna in the highest."

During Holy Week one year, I thought a lot about the Father even while contemplating the passion of Christ. Commemoration of the passion begins on Holy Thursday. St. Paul's First Epistle to the Corinthians 11:23-26 describes what happens on that night:

> "For I received from the Lord what I also handed on to you, that the Lord Jesus, on the night he was handed over, took bread, and after he had given thanks, broke it and said, 'This is my body that is for you. Do this in remembrance of me.' In the same way also the cup, after supper, saying, 'This cup is the new covenant in my blood. Do this, as often as you drink it, in remembrance of me.' For as often as you eat this bread and drink the cup, you proclaim the death of the Lord until he comes."

Something else happens at the Last Supper, illuminating the Son's relationship to the Father, which is read in the Gospel of John 13:1-15:

> "So, during supper, fully aware that the Father had put everything into his power and that he had come from God and was returning to God, he rose from supper and took off his outer garments. He took a towel and tied it around his waist. Then he poured water into a basin and began to wash the disciples' feet and dry them with the towel around his waist."

When Peter protests, Jesus tells him:

> "Unless I wash you, you will have no inheritance with me."

These are strong words that speak of loss of sonship, loss of place in God's Kingdom. The washing of the feet, along with the full awareness that the Father has put everything into his power, shows Jesus to be the one who cleanses his disciples of sin. Jesus reiterates here the power of forgiving sins which the Father gave him—a claim he made in public earlier and which led to accusations of blasphemy against him. The Gospel continues with a mandate to those who are present:

> "So when he had washed their feet [and] put his garments back on and reclined at table again, he said to them . . . 'If I, therefore, the master and teacher, have washed your feet, you ought to wash one another's feet. I have given you a model to follow, so that as I have done for you, you should also do.'"

I see on Holy Thursday two activities in which Christ is the model for his apostles. They are to become the first priests after Christ and will forgive sins and consecrate bread and wine, powers the Father puts into their hands *through Christ*.

These days, the washing of feet gets more attention than it did years ago. Each year a different group of people at my church is called upon to have their feet washed. At various times, they are the Altar Guild, the lay ministers, the teachers, or the helping hands of the church.

The washing of feet is, of course, a great sign of brotherly love, and especially, according to Jesus, it is a cleansing given by him alone. As such it supports the celebration of the Eucharist. It is still the Eucharist that holds the prime place in the liturgy, as I pay attention more keenly on this night to what I experience every time I go to Mass: partaking of the holy body and blood.

As the Mass on Holy Thursday evening ends, the priest carries the body of Jesus through the Church in procession to a side altar where it reposes until Easter. The tabernacle at St. Denis is empty and its alcove in darkness. The Lamb, whose icon in silver usually shines brightly on the brass door of the tabernacle, is not here.

This memorial of Holy Thursday night is infused with the knowledge of what happens next. Now darkness comes over the world as Christ leaves the fellowship of the Last Supper to go off in the night to pray to his Father—as it turns out, virtually alone, for no one stands by him.

This is the night of the Garden of Gethsemane.
This is the night of the beginning of Christ's torment.
He faces his tormentors alone.
He is dragged from one place to another,
Questioned and insulted by many,
And scourged repeatedly.
No one speaks to save the Son of Man,
The Lamb.
Master and teacher who washed their feet,
Who called them to Supper,
And gave them immortal food.

The next afternoon, Good Friday, I go to La Salette Shrine in Enfield, New Hampshire, for Stations of the Cross on the mountain overlooking Lake Mascoma. The climb up the mountainside is steep, and halfway up I rest on a bench. A La Salette priest passes on by, continuing to the top where the fourteen stations in white stone are profiled in the afternoon sky. By two o'clock the rest of the crowd arrives and each person makes the climb, some very slowly. It is one of those times when I feel I know the thoughts and feelings of other people.

About fifty people gather around the priest to say the Stations of the Cross. As three men carry a cross from one station to the next, the crowd follows behind them. The priest leads a meditation at each Station, and the people chant together the words of the thief crucified next to Christ in Luke 23:42: "Jesus, remember me when you come into your kingdom." When all is finished, we walk slowly back down the mountain behind the cross to the chapel, to reflect a little longer on the passion of Christ.

After awhile, the priest rises to speak briefly on the question: "Why did Christ have to suffer?" His community had discussed it in the morning and one person had offered this answer: "Because he said 'yes' to the Father."

Behind the question, I always think of another, implied question: Why would the Father have Christ suffer? Why would suffering and death be the path ordained by the Father for his Son? I think about this question a lot, and the priest's talk brings it back to me.

We do not always know the reason for the Father's will, only that his will is always good. Having said that, I think that the Father did not will his Son to suffer and die in this way. It is his nature to desire love and mercy, not hatred and condemnation. The "yes" that Christ gave to his Father was to remain true to his mission, and in this he was lovingly obedient, even to suffering and dying for it. It was men and women of free will who desired this death of Christ, and as St. Alphonse Liguori wrote for the first Station of the Cross centuries ago: "Lord, it was my sins that condemned Thee to die." The Passion of the Messiah was foretold and everyone was forewarned; but it was not foreordained by the Father.

I can think of any father saying to his son: "Son, always tell the truth." A son tries, but in being obedient begins to suffer for telling the truth. Then he may begin to lie to save himself. This was not Jesus. He told the truth always, even in the face of death. The truth he told was that the Father loves the world and that he, the Son, is the way to the Father and that he is one with the Father.

The La Salette Fathers are right. In light of the forces arrayed against him, Christ had to die because he said "yes" to the Father; that is, in my view, because he told the truth to all that he was the Son of the Father. After a public life of testifying to the truth, there was one last occasion when he would do so. It was now really a matter of life and death when the High Priest questioned him in Mark 14:61-62:

> "'Are you the Messiah, the son of the Blessed One?' Then Jesus answered, 'I am;
>> and "you will see the Son of Man
>>> seated at the right hand of the Power
>>> and coming with the clouds of heaven.'"
>
> At that the high priest tore his garments and said, 'What further need have we of witnesses? You have heard the blasphemy.'"

In saying "yes" to the Father, in telling the truth to the death, Christ brings us with him and lifts us up in the glory bestowed on him by his Father. There is a close union between the one who gives his life and the one for whom he gives it.

An example is the soldier who gives the supreme sacrifice of his life for his country. Oftentimes the sacrifice is foreseen, conscious, personal, and dedicated. On November 9, 2006, I read in Manchester, New Hampshire's *Union Leader* newspaper this account of the death of a 19-year-old Marine:

"'He said he needed to do this,' [his mother] recalled. 'He said if he could keep one dad from going to Iraq and he could take his place instead, then he'll feel like he's accomplished something.' His high school English teacher said that her student had seemed to know in high school what he was about. She found a poem he had written in her creative writing class: 'Many soldiers have had to experience the ultimate sacrifice,' he wrote. 'All you can do is hope that they finally found peace.'"

"He could take his place . . ." Taking another's place is at the heart of sacrifice. As the soldier stands in the place of one dad—or of me, or anyone—he reaches out and takes that one into his sacrifice. The soldier could rightly say to all of us: "I have won the victory for you. You are a people once again," and the people would know they have a part in the victory. It is perhaps something like this with Christ and his people.

Because Christ has saved us and taken us into his sacrifice, we can be so bold as to say with him, "*We* have won the victory. *We* are a people once again." In the final analysis, such a sacrifice is so astounding and is such a victory that, indeed, it must be the will of the Father.

As Easter dawns, the tabernacle at St. Denis is ablaze with light. The victorious Lamb of God has returned. Upon his icon on the door of the tabernacle, the Lamb carries a banner marked with the cross. He rests upon the scroll, sealed with the seven seals, which only he has the authority to open, releasing the demons of the world. He alone succeeds in the great task of overcoming the powers of evil and destruction in the world, as described in the Book of Revelation. And, as *He* is victorious, *we* are victorious.

12
EASTER AT ST. DENIS

"In union with the whole Church
we celebrate that day
when Jesus Christ, our Lord,
rose from the dead in his human body."
Eucharistic Prayer I for Easter
Magnificat, Holy Week 2006

Easter morning begins with a call from my friend Laura, telling
me that I need not bring Holy Communion to her husband at
their home as we had planned the night before. As a Eucharistic
minister to the homebound, I had wanted to make sure that Harry,
who is frail and in pain, had the opportunity to receive Communion
on Easter Sunday. But in the morning Harry really wants to try to
go to Mass. They plan to sit in the first pew, where the priest will
bring Communion to him.

St. Denis is crowded and from my view about seven rows back, I
have a small window on the Mass. I can see the paschal candle about
eight feet high in its stand and behind it a corner of the altar with
its white lace cloth and a sprig of forsythia arching over it. An altar
server brings the book, then later, at the offering prayers, replaces the
book with the cup. Behind the altar I can see the crucifix and above
that the stained glass windows bringing in the morning light. They
draw my gaze and invite me to look over the heads of everyone and
concentrate no matter how busy Mass gets.

Today the congregation, although at peak numbers, is reverent,
but even so, there are distractions. I decided some time ago that the
Mass is for the people—all of them—and I need to be mindful of
their presence. I am not in a cloister. Going to church is communal

as well as individual, and to be surrounded by the very young and the very old, I feel I can enter into their lives in this way. Everyone is here for a good reason, to celebrate the risen Lord; and some, like Harry, made a special effort to come.

There is a particular prayer in the Mass that is for everyone. It is the Eucharistic Prayer said aloud by the priest on behalf of the people. I think of it as the "people prayer," or the "Communion of Saints" prayer, because virtually everyone living and dead is remembered in it!

In the new Mass, the part called the Canon was renamed the Eucharistic Prayer. There are at least four different ones for ordinary Sundays and many others for special feast days like Easter. Spoken only by the priest following the *Sanctus,* the Eucharistic Prayer has many parts.

At times I find this prayer overly long when the sacredness of the Consecration is at hand. However, this is the time given to us to remember everyone for whom we want to pray, both the living and dead, starting with "ourselves and those who are dear to us."

There is a part of the Eucharistic Prayer called in Latin *"Communicantes"* from its first words: "In union with the whole church." At this time we honor Mary and Joseph, then the apostles and martyrs, and finally all the saints. All my life I have listened to the list of martyrs, but I haven't known anything about those whose names seem to speak of an early Christian world. Recently I looked up their names in the *Oxford Dictionary of Popes* and found that the first five were popes, as I suspected; the other martyrs I located in an old book of saints that belonged to my Grandmother Murphy. In the process, besides learning about the martyrs, I also learned something about the Canon of the Mass.

First the martyrs: Linus was the first successor of Peter as Bishop of Rome and thus considered to have been the second pope. His name occurs after Peter and Paul in the ancient Canon of the Mass. Cletus (short form of Anacletus) followed Linus as the third pope. He too was commemorated in the ancient Canon. Clement had personally known and worked with the apostles, authored an epistle, and was himself the fourth pope. Sixtus was the seventh pope and also listed in the Canon, while Cornelius was the twenty-second pope. Cornelius is known for his charity toward Christians who had denied their faith during imperial persecutions. He granted them readmission to the church after they had done penance. In records of the time, he "died gloriously" a euphemism for martyrdom.

The martyrdom of each of these popes, claimed by the Canon and by tradition, cannot be verified today. That in itself does not bother me, for the church's founding story was one of martyrdom—especially the martyrdom of Peter and Paul and many of the apostles. Those are verified in several sources, including the New Testament. The church is a suffering church in many times and places, and certainly this was so during the first three centuries.

I find the Canon to be very compelling testimony to the martyrdom of these popes, as well as others on the list: Cyprian, Bishop of Carthage; Lawrence, a Roman deacon; Chrysogonus; John and Paul, army officers; and Cosman and Damian, brothers who, according to another tradition, were bound and thrown into the sea during the persecution of Diocletian.

Now I have reason for a better appreciation of the Eucharistic Prayer, or Canon, which surrounds and contains the words of Consecration of the bread and wine. In this prayer we are given a long list of saints who shed their blood as Christ did, to testify to the truth who is the Father. Both the fledgling Church and the mature Church celebrate their sacrifice and their victory by placing their names close to the Eucharistic part of the Mass. And so we pray for them to remember us:

> "May their merits and prayers gain us your constant help and protection."

During the Eucharistic Prayer, I often think of the saints I have known, people I fervently believe are in the presence of God. Sometimes I silently put these and other names in my Eucharistic Prayer, when we honor "all the saints." This is simply based on my gratitude for those I have been blessed to know and from whom I have learned something valuable.

The first saint I ever knew was my Aunt Marie. In fact, she was so holy that her family "acclaimed" her sainthood. My mother, however, complained that she was a difficult person, while my father explained that saints were often like that—difficult, because they were different from the rest of us. Certainly Aunt Marie was different. She lived an austere life, continuing to follow the vows of poverty and chastity, which she had made as a cloistered Carmelite nun. In her elder years, she told me that she had difficulty with the vow of obedience in the convent and left for that reason.

She went from place to place to live, for awhile taking care of her elderly parents, until she moved to the home of a sister. The pleasures of life seemed to pass her by. Most of her adult life she did not appreciate efforts to help her live better. We did not realize that she was still, in her own soul, committed to her vows. If my mother gave her a sweater or robe or anything whatsoever, she would learn later that Aunt Marie had given it to the missions. Aunt Marie gave to the missions whatever came her way that she did not need. If she had two coats, she gave one away—as Christ once asked an aspiring disciple to do.

I became closer to her when I was a young married woman, and, as she aged, she actually became a more pleasant, happy person. When she died in a nursing home, true to her vows, she had very few belongings. One thing found in her room was a page she had written, titled: "What I am Thankful For," which one of my cousins read at her funeral:

"I am thankful to live here at St. Anne's where there is daily Holy Mass and Holy Communion offered. I am thankful for my nice bright room, for the lovely lamp and . . . for a comfortable bed. I'm thankful for the good food daily given us, for the kind waiters and waitresses and the housekeeper. . . . I'm thankful for my roommate who goes to bed early and is quiet. I'm thankful that I live in the U.S.A. where there is freedom of religion and I can vote. I'm thankful for our good Baptist President and for democratic government. I'm thankful for my continued good health. . . .

"I'm thankful for the kind nurses and aides, for good friends, and many others mostly in the craft classes, for the many entertainments, and for Bingo in which I've won many pretty and useful articles . . . and a $5 bill once. I'm thankful that we had Father Zahn as chaplain for years and for Father Jerry and all the priests helping us. There are likely other things that I can't think of now and have no more space. *Deo Gratias.*"

   In my personal Communion of Saints, Aunt Marie has a special niche. She had a complete love of God, and I am trusting that her life of beatitude and gratitude will continue to inspire me. Other people, in addition to my family, have been wonderful examples without their ever knowing it.

   Among the people of St. Denis I will always remember Rilla, a friend who radiated love and biblical faith. When we studied the fourth chapter of the Gospel of John together, she told us how she loved the story of the Samaritan woman who is drawing still water from a well when Jesus comes along and tells her, ". . . whoever drinks the water I shall give will never thirst." One day after this Gospel was read, Rilla and I saw each other at some distance on our way out of church. We broke into smiles, each knowing the other marveled to hear again the story of the encounter of Christ and the woman. Rilla and her husband Walter live on at St. Denis in my memory and, more importantly, in the memory of the whole Church in the great Eucharistic Prayer.

   But I have living friends on their way to being saints, and I also think of them in the Eucharistic Prayer. Among those who are dear to me is Elaine. We met at La Salette Shrine, where I was covering a story for the local newspaper. Since Elaine lives most of the year in New York City, our friendship was forged mostly through correspondence—for me the first that was mainly religious in nature. She responded to any question or problem I set forth, as in this letter: "You mentioned that your bible group had been focusing on the Son of Man. I suspect the day's leader may already have turned up Pope John Paul's piece on that subject—like all the talks in his series on Jesus, this one is so complete and so marvelous." She enclosed a copy of "Jesus Christ, Son of Man" from the Pope's general audience (April 29, 1987). Actually, we had not turned up this resource on our own.

   I have a good-sized box filled with art postcards, book reviews, and article clippings, even encyclicals accompanying Elaine's letters. For twenty years, she has led me gently into a new realm of Catholic thought, beyond my Catholic basics and even beyond the bible study

I had come to think of as constituting my growth as a Catholic. As a Shakespeare scholar, Elaine has assets that I lack, and she has developed her own way of what I think of as praying art, praying literature, and praying the liturgical year.

One Sunday during the Easter season we met after Mass and she spoke of how she was looking forward to Pentecost the next Sunday. Now I was vaguely aware that Pentecost was approaching but had not given it special thought. For Elaine, each Mass is a part of the full life of Christ in the liturgical year which she not only observes when it comes around—but anticipates. I recently reread some notes she made "On the liturgical year" which she shared with me years ago:

> "Each year you actually experience what Jesus went through—for you. It's not that it all happened 2,000 years ago and is over and done with. It happened for you. And you have to respond. So, early in the year, you read a book like Romano Guardini's *The Lord*—Guardini has the ability of making you see all of the familiar events in Christ's life in a fresh and deeper way. Or during Lent you read Barbet's *A Doctor at Calvary* and you find out what a crucifixion was really like. Or, after Easter, you concentrate on the growth of the Church—Augustine , Aquinas, Bede Jarrett's life of Dominic, the autobiography of Therese of Lisieux, Bernard Ruffin's biography of Padre Pio. It's a study of the infinite you are making—and the resourcess are inexhaustible."

Another special friend is Melanie, my "godchild" who became a Catholic in her eighties. We met when she was considering the Catholic faith after many years without religious affiliation. Through her adult life, her own great bent for matters of the spirit had drawn her in other directions. I could try to help her with some Catholic questions, but she became a mentor to me as well. Blessed with good health in her old age, she continually extends her love to others, especially our nursing home residents whom she feared did not have sufficient spiritual aid. Her response was to bring them the rosary, and so for some years now there has come about a multi-faith group, praying every Monday to God through Melanie's beloved "Mother Mary."

Like Aunt Marie, I am thankful for all my good friends and in a special way for my Catholic friends. We are drawn to each other in the Communion of Saints with Our Lord, and now and forever help one another to know him and to love him.

As this particular Easter Mass ends, Laura and Harry are still sitting in the front pew as everyone else is getting up to leave. Harry's face is gleaming as I go over to wish them a happy Easter.

"I've never sat so close to it all before," he says. "This was just beautiful."

And I think: "They don't want this to end." The good news is: It does not end. Jesus Christ, our Lord, is risen. *Alleluia. Alleluia.*

13

JOHN PAUL II, I LOVE YOU

"This is my body."
Consecration, Eucharistic Prayer 1
Magnificat

I used to wonder what it would be like to be with thousands of people in St. Peter's Square and to see the Holy Father, whoever he might be at the time, come to his window and give his blessing and a few words to the crowd. I have a photo of my father in one of those crowds reaching out to touch John Paul II in his open car. That was in the early days of his papacy before the Pope was shot and gravely injured in St. Peter's Square.

And then one day I was in Rome, crossing St. Peter's Square and climbing the stairs to the Pope's own chapel for his early morning Mass. I was able to be with him in prayer and to personally greet him when it was over. This opportunity came about soon after Virg and I retired, during the pontificate of John Paul II during the Great Jubilee of the Year 2000. It surpassed anything I ever imagined.

Our invitation to attend his daily Mass was extended by John Paul II himself through Teresa, our friend and fellow parishioner. We pilgrims were aware that this special privilege came to us because Teresa was a friend of His Holiness. On a visit to Rome, she told the Pope about our parish study group that was preparing for the celebration of the Jubilee year. He was pleased, and on hearing of our plans for a pilgrimage to Rome, he reportedly said, "Why don't you come to my Mass?"

"Why don't you come to my Mass?" The words were so simple. When I first heard of them, they seemed like words that Christ might say. Words of invitation like "Come and see," to those who wanted to know him better.

The day of our Mass in the Pope's chapel dawned for me after a sleepless night in a convent where our little group of St. Denis pilgrims was staying. I had been comfortable but too excited about the next day to sleep. We had to rise early on this January morning and leave the convent while it was still dark. We were more quiet than usual when we boarded our bus at 6:15 a.m. It usually dropped us off several blocks from our destination, but this morning the bus drove through the Vatican gates right onto St. Peter's Square. Our pastor, Father Steve, wearing his new cassock for the second day and carrying his white chasuble, led us in prayer before we stepped out onto the stones of St. Peter's.

Later, my fellow pilgrims Dotty and Marty remembered "the dawn coming up, St. Peter's Basilica, the Christmas tree with its lights still on, and the stars still visible in the sky. The only sound was the clatter of our footsteps as we hurried expectantly across the cobblestones toward the chapel of the Holy Father!" Their words said it all.

The Pope was at his kneeler praying, his back to us as we entered his chapel. Behind his kneeler was his chair that appeared to be made of bronze, and on the back of the chair, facing us, were cast the words of the *Pater Noster*. He seemed at first sight such a familiar figure, an old friend.

"When he prays, he physically folds into himself and disappears into a deeper realm," our choir director, Sheila, later recalled. Father Steve said he would always remember the awe of entering the Pope's chapel and seeing him on his knees praying. "It was what you had always heard about, that he is a man of prayer, but there we were, praying with him," he said.

After a few minutes, the Pope rose to be vested by two assistants and Father Steve donned his white chasuble to celebrate Mass with the Pope. The Mass began and proceeded as it always does. Father Steve could assist the Pope as he would any other priest, anywhere in the world. The Pope spoke parts of the Mass in English and some in Latin as he faced the altar which was built against a wall of red marble, where at his eye level there was a small icon of his beloved Our Lady of Czestohowa with the Infant Jesus. I appreciated that we all faced the same direction with the Pope, *ad orientam,* toward Christ, the Light of the World.

I looked over his familiar back, very bent by age and illness and hard work, as he took the bread and wine into his hands and said the words of Consecration. The whole body of the Pope, bent over these gifts of human hands, was prayerful, reverent, sacrificial. And then, invoking the power of the Holy Spirit, he said what all priests say:

"The day before he suffered . . ."

When these words come in the middle of the long Eucharistic Prayer, the Consecration is at hand. These five words are very specific in time and intent. Christ is at supper with his twelve apostles the day before he dies, and he leaves his last will, their inheritance as it were, to his apostles.

"he took bread in his sacred hands . . ."

On all their travels to towns along dusty roads, many times these twelve men must have seen Christ take bread into his hands. The priest also, each time he offers Mass, takes in his hands a host of flat bread, holding it over the cup, and bending low while he says:

"and looking up to heaven, to you his almighty Father, he gave you thanks and praise."

The prayer of Christ at this supper is essentially the same as we pray at the beginning of the Eucharistic Prayer I—"We come to you, Father, with praise and thanksgiving." It reminds me that it is rightly the Father to whom prayer is directed, and praise and thanksgiving are the best attitudes of prayer. But it is unfathomable that one could praise and thank God when facing up to an unjust and inhumane death. Only by Christ's example can I know there is such a state of prayer. I know that Christ will ask the Father later that evening in the garden to let this cup of suffering pass from him. The Father is mute here, so it would seem. Yet the Son knows the Father and the Father knows the Son. Their will is one.

"He broke the bread,"

No doubt the apostles are also accustomed to seeing Christ break a loaf of bread and pass it around the table for all to share, together to draw life and strength from it. At Mass, after the Consecration is complete, the priest breaks what has become the body of Christ. Often at Mass I hear the snap of it as the priest breaks the Sacred Host, and I think now that Christ's breaking of the bread at the Last Supper foreshadows that his body will also be broken.

"gave it to his disciples, and said, 'Take this, all of you, and eat it.'"

Christ gives first to these twelve chosen men what he offers to the Father, and it is to be eaten by *all* of them. They perhaps see similarities to some of the sacrifices of the Jewish priesthood in which the priests consumed offerings.

"This is my body which will be given up for you."

Ah, this is new. Bread becomes body, to be given up for them. What begins as bread, broken and shared at a meal, with these words becomes Christ's body, broken and given up for them. What he takes in his sacred hands becomes his offering of his own sacred life.

"When supper was ended he took the cup. Again he gave you thanks and praise, gave the cup to his disciples, and said: 'Take this, all of you, and drink from it: This is the cup of my blood, the blood of the new and everlasting covenant.'"

The entire life of Christ expresses a new covenant of love and self-sacrifice, and now God gives us everything. Although in the past, he fulfilled promises of land, children, laws, and blessings, now he gives that most precious gift of his Son.

"It will be shed for you and for all so that sins may be forgiven."

Shortly after the Last Supper his blood begins to be shed. Christ leaves this supper among friends to go to the garden where he is arrested. During the night he is scourged, and again in the morning before the cross is placed on his back. More blood is shed as he is whipped along the Way of the Cross, falling and forced to rise again and again. Finally, when he reaches the mount, he is nailed through his arms and feet to this instrument of execution. When at last he is about to die, there is scarcely any blood left in his body when the soldier puts a lance into his side. His is the sacred blood that fills the chalices of the world. I would not profane the sacred body by eating it, nor the sacred blood by drinking it, except that Christ says to his disciples: "eat," and "drink," and then:

"Do this in memory of me."

The pope and every priest descend from those apostles who watched and listened closely to Christ that night. The priest says and does essentially what the gospels tell us Christ said and did on the night before he died. Christ told his apostles he would shed his blood for them "and for all" so that sins may be forgiven. Now *we* are the "all" by *his* own words of offering.

The small, round, white Sacred Host which the Pope raised in his hands over his head that morning in Rome looked just as it did a few moments earlier, but it was not the same. Most of my life I have been aware of this mystery which I learned a long time ago is called "transubstantiation"—that in the words and actions of Christ the substance of the bread is changed into his body and the wine into his blood. Once I looked up "substance" in the dictionary. The substance of a thing is what makes it what it really is. Substance can be physical, as in the material of a thing; and it can be abstract, as in the meaning of a story, a claim, a law, a life. I like to think of substance as the heart of the matter. At the heart of the matter of the Consecration is the real meaning of the real suffering body of Christ.

The Pope on this day was experiencing his own real suffering, just as at the Consecration, symbol and metaphor die away in the face of the very real. For a moment I was amazed when the frail Pope knelt almost to the floor on one knee after raising the Sacred Body and Blood for us to adore. Then I realized that this man would not spare himself in this or any other way as long as he lived. When he knelt, I could see that the soles of his shoes were quite worn and that he seemed to be wearing some sort of bandages around his legs, and these kept slipping down beneath his robes. What a bother that would be. My heart went out to him.

The effect the Holy Father had on me in his private chapel is not really unlike the effect any priest has at Mass, any place in the world it is offered. Every priest is there in the person of Christ. To know that the priest is there in the person of Christ, saying the words of Christ, and that he is ordained for this sacrifice since the time of the apostles, means that it really makes no difference whether he is the pope or the parish priest. Even so, certain priests in their own demeanor evoke something special in my soul. The Pope was such a priest.

Since God accepts these gifts which we offer with the priest and he consecrates, they are substantially who God is. Now I see: God is, who is given up for me. When I was a child, I learned to say, "My Lord and my God," at the Consecration of the bread and wine. Through all the years, I have not been able to think of a better prayer for this moment, unless it is silence.

While God remains a white wafer to my sight, the priest helps me to see God. I may be face-to-face with the priest across the altar, as in my own church; or I may see the mystery unfold over the bent back and then the raised arms of the Pope, as I did in Rome. I know that a priest gives all that he is to stand and kneel and raise his arms at the altar in the great presentation of the Body and Blood of Christ: to make Christ present in this way that Christ willed to be. And then he prays:

> "Through him, with him, in him, in the unity of the Holy
> Spirit, all glory and honor is yours, almighty Father, forever
> and ever."

Long before I saw the Holy Father offer Mass in person, I watched him raise his arms in blessings to the world he greatly loved. Then one day, those same arms brought Christ to me. John Paul II, I love you! *Requiescat in pace!*

Just a year before the Great Jubilee of the Year 2000, I was fortunate to receive a copy of the premiere issue of *Magnificat* in the United States. This monthly missal arrived in the mailbox in time for the celebration of Advent, in preparation for Christmas 1998. The first thing that struck me was the title *Magnificat* from the famous canticle of Mary: "My soul magnifies the Lord," which is in the Confraternity edition of the bible. It is now translated in the New American Bible, "My soul proclaims the greatness of the Lord." Next, the reproduction of a beautiful painting of "The Virgin Mother with Child" on the cover. Surely, John Paul II, in his own love for the Mother with Child, was pleased with the title and everything inside this new pocket-sized monthly missal, first published in French and now in English as well.

Between the covers of this first issue were all the prayers of the Mass for the month of December; an abbreviated Liturgy of the Hours for morning and evening prayers; blessings, litanies, and hymns; and short articles on liturgy and scripture. One of my immediate favorite sections was "Meditation of the Day." There was a different author for each day of the month, from the Fathers of the Church to Dorothy Day, Annie Dillard, and T.S. Eliot. There were current church fathers such as Joseph Ratzinger and Christophe Schonborn; and Saints Gregory the Great, John of the Cross, and Therese of Lisieux. Sometimes "Meditation of the Day" featured Catholic poets, and I loved the poem titled "Advent" by the twentieth-century Carmelite Jessica Powers that begins: "I live my Advent in the Womb of Mary."

Last but not least was the final section of *Magnificat*—several pages devoted to a painting by Georges de la Tour, titled "The Newborn." Never had I seen such a glistening newborn Jesus in art, and the text describing the painting was clearly written by an expert in sacred art.

As a personal missal and prayer book *Magnificat* is a treasure, but there is an abundant choice of personal missals including Latin ones which, happily in my view, are making a comeback. As for *Magnificat*, which I know best, it is a joy to look at, to read, to learn from, and to pray the Mass by each day of the month. The great prayer of the Mass is always up-to-date liturgically, while many traditional prayers are brought forward. It is a small book but a great gift to the Church and to the world at the beginning of the third millenium of Christianity, when we are called to the New Evangelization, so close to the loving heart of John Paul II.

14

SUPPER IN THE KINGDOM

"Thy Kingdom come; thy will be done
on earth as it is in heaven."

The Lord's Prayer
Magnificat

O rder is built into the Mass, as its prayers and actions proceed
within a grand design to a high point for a purpose. In that
way it is like Scripture, as God's plan is revealed from creation to
redemption and on to the coming of the Kingdom of God.

When the Lord's Prayer, the Our Father, comes soon after the
priest has said the words of consecration in the Mass, it always seems
to me somewhat out of place. Such a familiar, everyday prayer as the
Our Father does not seem especially Eucharistic at this moment,
so shortly before we receive Holy Communion. Perhaps earlier in
the Mass—somewhere amid the blessing, confession, praise and
thanksgiving prayers—it would fit better. I really need to think
more about this prayer which I say every day and every time I am
at Mass.

Certainly the Our Father is a sublime, short prayer that comes to
us from the lips of Christ himself. He does not quote any patriarch,
prophet, or psalmist when he tells his disciples not to babble as the
pagans do, for "Our Father knows what you need before you ask
him." His admonition is a key to his prayer that follows in Matthew
6:7-13. He says to his disciples:
"So you should pray like this.
'Our Father, who art in heaven,
hallowed be thy name;
thy Kingdom come,

thy will be done on earth
as it is in heaven.
Give us this day our daily bread;
and forgive us our trespasses
as we forgive those who trespass against us;
and lead us not into temptation,
but deliver us from evil.'"

"Our Father, who art in heaven, hallowed be thy name."

First, we are invited—along with Christ—to call upon Our
Father in heaven—the Father that Jesus has until now called *my*
Father. Christ gives his Father to us by name, as we are his children.
Our Father is in heaven, but what/where is heaven? For now, I just
think: Heaven is that state of being in which Our Father comes to
us. It is his Kingdom.

"Thy Kingdom come, thy will be done on earth as it is in
heaven."

These words indicate that we are to pray that his Kingdom comes
by doing his will here and now. I believe that is what the prayer of
Christ puts upon my lips to say and upon my life to do. Its goal, to
achieve on earth the perfection of heaven, seems to me impossible.
Yet the prayer itself is an antidote to despair, for contained in its
words are meanings that speak of eternity. First, heaven itself is our
very real model; and second, the Kingdom is always coming.

In the *Catechism of the Catholic Church*, I found this magnificent
line: "The Kingdom of God has been coming since the Last Supper,
and, in the Eucharist, it is in our midst." (#2816) This one line helps
me understand better the Kingdom of God and hence the entire
Lord's Prayer. It further sheds light on why it comes in the most
solemn, Eucharistic part of the Mass.

When Christ prays, "Thy Kingdom come," he himself is the
one who will bring about this new beginning for the people of God.
It is indeed striking that the *Catechism* pinpoints the beginning of
the coming of the Kingdom of God in our time to the events of the
Last Supper. There Christ offered himself in his body and blood, in
actual and eternal sacrifice, a sign that in the sweeping redemption

that soon followed, the Kingdom of God is evermore present and always coming.

I can see a little more of heaven now, in this Kingdom that "has been coming since the Last Supper." It is the glory of Our Father reigning with the Son and the Holy Spirit in each heart, on each altar, where his name is being hallowed and his will is being done. But it still seems clear from the words of Christ that he will yet deliver the world from evil once and for all. While we await that final deliverance, the past, the present, and the future are all rolled into this one prayer. It is in itself a prayer that expresses the eternity in which God lives, and he is already sharing it with us.

"Give us this day our daily bread and forgive us our
trespasses as we forgive those who trespass against us."

Here is language that is very clear about what we are to do. It sounds a lot like the commandment of Christ: "Love your neighbor as I have loved you." In each case, I am to be *as* Christ to others! To love *as* Christ loves me. To forgive *as* Christ forgives me. Forgiveness is an aspect of love, divine love on permanent loan, since it goes so against the human grain. How else could I get over the hurts that come to me? And how else could I make myself into a new person who never wants to hurt back?

"Lead us not into temptation but deliver us from evil."

These are strong words, but I need to know what I am up against and call it by its name. I usually think of my own life as pretty serene, but there are exceptions. Surprisingly, one exception occurred the Sunday after Christmas one year, on the Feast of the Holy Family. That day Father Kevin had spoken about how in our society so many families are at odds with each other (I always think, whew, that's not us). He had described the Holy Family as a family under stress but one that is a model for us of protective love. The priest had advised families to forgive and have mercy.

In this way I was approaching the new year, with thoughts of holy families, on a morning when I was very tired but immensely grateful not to have become ill or overstressed during my daughter Brenda's Christmas visit. Her last visit, eighteen months before, had been marred in a way that I felt it took until now for us to get over completely. For some time, I had dwelt on this problem of lingering hurt feelings between my daughter and me, even in the aftermath of apologies. We had still needed a good visit, and we had just had one.

I was also touched by the priest's kind remarks to a congregation significantly smaller than that of Christmas. He called us faithful for coming back on this feast day and prayed God to bless us for our faithfulness. What with Christmas, my daughter's visit, our reunion in forgiveness, and my husband by my side, I was feeling a warm glow all over. Although we shared Christmas Mass with Brenda, my husband and I were back to being alone, a situation that has both its sorrows and its comforts. Sorrow that we share such little time with our children and grandchildren; yet happiness, knowing they are faith-filled, well and happy, loving and being loved.

With such feelings of well being and gratitude, it came as such a surprise when, after leaving church, my husband brought up a subject which quickly led to a hurtful exchange between the two of us. I know my own tendency to speak carelessly at times, and I may have unwittingly added fuel to this fire. Perhaps I was hurt and angry because at that moment I had been so happy. I could not believe this sudden change in my sense of well being, because minutes before I had heard the words of the priest about the Holy Family and I had made such a renewed personal commitment to my family and been assured of such strength and blessing.

And yet strength and blessing did come to me. Later I could see that I was delivered from evil, one that would have taken the form of a new grievance in my heart toward one I love. It did not take long to get over this. Perhaps because of the personal commitment I had made at Mass that day, I would not harbor any resentment toward my husband as I had my daughter. I would not shackle myself to that post so soon again. Later on, I wrote in my journal: "My way is to go forward to the next Mass—and the next—and so on, as my salvation is gained step by step, day by day. Mass is memory."

I don't remember now exactly what I meant by that last sentence. I think I meant that Mass is first of all a memory Christ gave to us of his loving sacrifice for us, freeing us from sin and drawing us closer to Our Father. That is the kind of memory I want, and in this case memory of my own release that day from a stubborn sin. Blessedly,

I would not be led into another temptation that same day. I would be delivered from evil.

All of this leads me to understand that the Lord's Prayer is not a blueprint for human achievement. Of course we are called to participate in the ongoing coming of the Kingdom, but we ourselves cannot make it happen. Even so, God does not give us impossible missions. He is with us always, until the end of time. The surest way he is with us is at Mass, in the Eucharist.

Early in his ministry on earth, Christ began to speak on the mountain to the people about Our Father. From the Cross, he hallowed his name. He brought his Kingdom down to earth. He did Our Father's will. He defeated Satan—who held the living and the dead in his grasp—so that people who are destined for God are no longer separated from his fullness.

The Lord's Prayer is a Eucharistic prayer after all, for it is Christ, his Son, who has been coming down from heaven all these years since the Last Supper, bringing his body, Our Father's Kingdom—all that is his—into our midst, right into enemy territory. Christ is my heaven, and I really do nothing to make him so, except to be present, unworthy as I am, for him to enter my roof. And that is in the next part of the Mass.

The Our Father is soon followed by the *Agnus Dei,* another prayer of simple majesty, as Holy Communion approaches. The priest breaks the Sacred Host just as the Gospels of Matthew, Mark, and Luke say that Jesus broke the bread. Then the priest drops a small piece of it into the cup, reuniting the Body and Blood of Jesus, a sign of his resurrection. All the while, the people pray together, three times calling out "Lamb of God" in the words of John the Baptist in John 1:29, when he first sees Jesus: "Behold, the Lamb of God, who takes away the sin of the world." With these words John introduced Jesus to the world by the title that speaks of the gentle, spotless, innocent sacrifices of old, and to which he added implicitly the action of redeemer.

Finally, in the last action of the priest before Holy Communion, he holds up the Body of Jesus to the people and says:

"This is the Lamb of God, who takes away the sins of the world. Happy are those who are called to his supper."

And each person replies:

"Lord, I am not worthy to receive you, but only say the word and my soul shall be healed."

I always think of a slightly different response in the Latin Mass, for which the English translation is:

"Lord, I am not worthy that you should come under my roof; say but the word and my soul shall be healed."

These words follow more closely the faith-filled words of the Roman centurion in Luke 7:6-7. The image of a person like the centurion, an outsider, thinking himself to be unworthy that the Lord should come under his roof, is a powerful one. As Holy Communion approaches, and the Lord comes under *my* roof, I think that he fulfills—he *is*—"thy Kingdom come." He is the wheat gathered into my barn. He is my sheltering tree, my leavened bread, my field of treasure, and my fine pearl.

15
Anima Christi

"Soul of Christ, sanctify me."

St. Ignatius Loyola

In May one year, my husband and I traveled to Minneapolis for our grandson Jack's First Communion. I had in my luggage four books for Jack, who is an avid reader. He likes history, adventure, and mystery, and after much back-and-forth I had finally chosen four lives of the saints for children. All of these lives had great adventure, and they all left their mark in history: St. John Bosco, the apostle of youth; St. Francis of Assisi, who gave up all earthly goods; Father Damien, who lived with the lepers of Molokai; and Mother Cabrini, the Italian nun who helped immigrants in America. There is a story in the family that Virg's great-grandfather Angelo was a friend and patron of Mother Cabrini in New York City, so I passed this bit of lore along to Jack in our inscription of the book.

Jack has always been such a kind child, and I marvel at this gift in him which we could see from his earliest years. His mother says that he wants to please and is sorry when he has done something wrong. He is sociable and attuned to the feelings of others. From the time he was a baby until he started school all day, he went with his mother to her morning rosary group once a week. First it was just Jack and his mother, later Julianne, Tommy, and Noelle came along, joining the other kids who played together while their mothers prayed. His parents also took him with them, from the time he was a few months old, to deliver Meals on Wheels in a nearby neighborhood. Once he could walk, he went up to the doors with his mother to deliver the meals. Sheila told me that the elderly, homebound people often said they were so happy to see a young child because they seldom do anymore.

During our visit in Minneapolis I wondered what Jack thought about his upcoming First Communion for which he had prepared all year. On the Sunday before Jack's big day, another boy had his First Communion at St. Joseph's Church. This plan of individual First Communion, I learned, is yet another new way to do things! Instead of receiving the sacrament for the first time as a class, each child does so on a date chosen by each family. Jack's date, I knew, hinged on our ability to travel to Minneapolis, and supposedly other families chose their dates for such reasons.

On this particular Sunday, the Feast of the Ascension, to my surprise a lay preacher gave the homily. She talked about what it means for Jesus to be present in our lives since he is not physically present to us as he was to his disciples. If Jesus had not ascended into heaven, and if he were still here in his human body, she supposed that we would likely seek him out for personal advice and thus not grow spiritually as we now must do. Now, the Spirit makes him present to us, in our hearts. We see him, in our hearts. We hear him, she said, in our hearts.

At the end, Jack said to me, "Very interesting." I was amazed that he followed the homily; then on the way out of church he said that he had not really understood it. I needed to think about it myself, and I hoped we could talk about it some more during the week. We should have seized that moment!

Tom and Sheila had on their coffee table a little book by Henri Nouwen, titled *With Burning Hearts,* given by their church to all the parents of the First Communicants. I started to read this meditation on the Eucharist, told as a personal account by Father Nouwen. As I read on, it seemed an excellent book and a good choice for parents' own inspiration.

It is odd though, how difficult it is to find a time to talk about God. Prayer is a given; and it is given certain times in our lives. For example, in Sheila's family, at the beginning of every meal they say grace, followed by Tom saying, "All for Jesus." Prayers with the children at night are another time. I noticed that the older children, who started out with "God, bless Mommy and Daddy . . . ," have now learned the basic Catholic prayers: the Our Father, Hail Mary, Glory Be, and Apostles Creed, which they say at bedtime.

In between times, there is everything else in life. This week, it was multiple soccer games; shopping and cleaning for the party on Sunday; trips to nurseries, shopping centers, furniture stores; visits to parks and museums; attending the school picnic and field day; games and reading with the kids; preparing meals and doing dishes.

I really wanted to talk to Jack about First Communion. Nouwen in his book writes of the Eucharist as an "invitation," and I thought if I picked up on that idea, maybe I could ask Jack if he knew that he could talk to Jesus about anything when Jesus comes to him. And so at that moment, as I was reading Nouwen's book, I called to him to see if he could come to the living room, but—in a way that did not seem like Jack—he just went on his way.

So I went back to the book, only to come across Father Nouwen's comment that it is harder to talk about God with those closest to us than with strangers. With Jack, I felt that he knew what I was up to, and he wasn't going for it!

The next Sunday morning all eight of us were up early to eat breakfast, put together the platters of food for the party, bathe and dress, and arrive at the church on time. There we met a friendly, retired priest who was filling in for the day. He was thrilled to have Jack receive his First Communion on his day there and told Jack he remembered his own First Communion. The first three rows were reserved for the Brandes family, and many of Tom's brothers, sisters, nieces and nephews, and his mother and stepfather were already there.

At the offering of the gifts, Tom, Sheila, and Jack brought up the cups containing the soon-to-be-consecrated bread and wine. Jack's sister, Julianne, who will do this in two years, was excited, singing all the hymns and almost dancing out of her seat. When it was time to receive the sacrament, Jack and his parents walked onto the altar and the priest gave the three of them Holy Communion together for the first time. It must have been very special for these parents to do this with him alone, to be with him alone—in a sense like they were when he was their only child before their love would multiply four times. Jack was in the center between them, just under the skylight, and as this Sunday was the Feast of Pentecost, I could almost "see" that great Christian symbol of the dove coming to hover over his head.

On this day Jack received not only the Body of Christ, he received the grace of the Holy Spirit. I believe he will always be a God-loving person and be among the blessed. At first he was a little apprehensive, but once things were underway he seemed to be secure. Indeed, he is secure always, in having the Bread of Life come to him.

I know that I feel more secure than ever in my life, even with lengthening age. In everything that happens, God's grace in the Mass helps me. It also helps me approach the needs of other people who are ill or handicapped. One of these was Al.

One year Al appeared at bible study. At the time I did not know him, nor did I pay much attention to him that first year. He was quiet and sat at the end of the table. Then I began to see him around town, often standing at the edge of the road, looking up to the sky. Or slowly walking the three blocks between church and his home. Others in bible study sometimes brought him a bag of cookies or gave him a ride home on a bad day. His unfailing attendance at bible study, even with his poor health and in the worst weather, said to me that he was a needy and lonely person. Sometimes we wondered what to do about Al. I remember my friend Cathy saying, "We know what Mother Teresa would do."

Our new pastor, Father Steve, was the kind of person to address any problem, and he called a meeting of the town social worker, the police chief, a psychiatrist, and a few people from the parish who wanted to help Al. Of several things that were wrong, one very noticeable one was that Al didn't seem to bathe and wash his clothes regularly. At our meeting that day, we decided that we could help the situation by doing his laundry. I offered to ask him about it and to do the laundry if he would cooperate.

But even approaching someone to ask about something so personal was a huge hurdle for me. As it turned out, Al was agreeable to being helped, saying that it was hard for him to walk down to the basement in his home to do the laundry. Once "project laundry" was underway, it caused me much unease each time that I did it. I found the best help to be this: Go to morning Mass on laundry day. Offer this work to God. Pray for the strength and the right attitude to do it.

The last part was the hardest, but over time I learned something about the human person and the human body. If I were a doctor or nurse, I'd probably have learned it a lot sooner. We can have nothing but love for the human person and the human body even in its most unpleasant forms—and as it turns out, our clothes bear all these signs of the living, human body.

In Holy Communion, I can imagine the Body of Christ as it was during his suffering and dying: bloody, dirty, wounded, smelly. Now, the memorial of his Body is a clean affair for us, but entering into his sacrifice is to know that the human body in his likeness is all those things as well. The human body is everywhere, and it continues to suffer and die, but in the case of this one man, I thought I should try for once in my life to try to be like one who wipes the face of Jesus or one who anoints his feet with ointment.

I would also like to tell Jack about the prayer I learned for my First Communion, the "Prayer before a Crucifix." Although Holy Communion is a time to talk to Jesus in our own words, a formal, appropriate prayer like this one begins to direct the mind to contemplate the wounded Body of Christ.

In this prayer, which is in Chapter One, several phrases offer images for contemplation: "kind and most sweet Jesus," "thy five most precious wounds," and the words of David: "They *pierced* my hands and my feet. They have *numbered* all my bones."

When I was a child, the only person I knew who had suffered was Jesus. Only when I was an adult did I begin to use these last words—"They have numbered all my bones"—to pray for people who by then I knew were, like Christ, suffering immensely. Indeed suffering people often have so many afflictions piling one on top of the other that it must seem to them that all their bones have been numbered.

But in the first part of the "Prayer Before a Crucifix" are the words: "I cast myself on my knees in thy sight," and "impress upon my heart lively sentiments of faith, hope, and charity, with true repentance for my sins. . . ." Such a prayer after Holy Communion is a reminder of my very real redemption by Christ, who offers me a life of revitalized virtue and all the means to turn away from sin and the will of the self over God—the *original* cause of all suffering.

Surely the Body of Christ that I receive in Holy Communion is healing, mending, recreating, pulsing life through my body. The Body of Christ in its perfect physical presence joins my own imperfect body, and my body, I believe, responds to this perfect Body. My body answers in its own created ways that are not exactly known to me. It is as if my body answers directly to its Creator, who is perfection. The weaknesses of my body do not necessarily disappear. They may get better, they may stay the same, or they may get worse; yet my body is *better* for its encounter with God.

My soul also responds to its Creator, when the Body of Christ comes to me. My soul becomes more like my original soul as first brought into being by the mind of God—all good, all-praising, all-loving. And so my soul, like my body, leaps at the call of its Creator, who is now also its Redeemer. This is possible only because Christ gave all of himself to make my soul new again.

These days I also say another classic prayer, *"Anima Christi"* by St. Ignatius Loyola, following Holy Communion. I only learned it many years after "The Prayer before a Crucifix," and I find that *"Anima Christi"* also brings to mind a contemplation of Jesus in his passion.

"Soul of Christ, sanctify me.
Body of Christ, save me.
Blood of Christ, inebriate me.
Water from the side of Christ, wash me.
Passion of Christ, strengthen me.
O good Jesus, hear me.
Within your wounds, shelter me.
Never permit me to be separated from you.
From the evil one, protect me.
In the hour of my death, call me.
And bid me come to you.
That with your saints I may praise you.
Forever and ever. Amen."

This list of entreaties begins with calling upon the Soul, the most fundamental part of the identity and individuality of each person, including Christ himself. And so I say:

"Soul of Christ, sanctify me." Make my soul holy.

"Body of Christ, save me." Deliver me from evil.

"Blood of Christ, inebriate me." Make me forget myself as a drunkard does, as a martyr does. Put limits on my desire to preserve myself.

"Water from the side of Christ, wash me." Clean me totally only with what is left of you on the Cross, the water that spurts from your pierced side.

"Passion of Christ, strengthen me." Make me strong even as you lose your own strength.

These few lines of "Anima Christi" show me how such a formal prayer is a means for forging prayer in the heart, just when I most want to talk to Jesus and cannot think of anything special—or worthy of him—to say. In this prayer, I tell him that I completely rely upon him. Only he can make me holy. Only he can save me. Only he can make me forget myself. And only he can make me strong.

16
DEO GRATIAS

"The Mass is ended. Go in peace."
"Thanks be to God."

Dismissal B
Magnificat

Father Steve, who left our church to become pastor of a large one in the southern part of the state, came back one day to our area for a special occasion. He was the main celebrant and homilist for a Mass which Virg and I and some of his other former parishioners attended. That night he told a story about a priest who went to Africa as a missionary. One wet and muddy Sunday, the missionary was surprised that the people had come to church on such a bad day. "O Father," they said to him, "every day is a good day. The Lord is always good. It is his nature."

They might also have said, "Every Mass is a good Mass," for it was the reason for their seemingly effortless joy. Such faith shines out in thankfulness for a Lord who is good by his nature and gives us a memory of himself all the days of our lives.

After Father Steve's Mass and the reception that followed, I experienced the completion not only of a ritual but a sense of my soul "filled up" with grace. As Virg and I left the reception on a very dark night just as rain began to fall, I turned back to Father Steve and said, "Father, every day is a good day," and he quickly replied, "The Lord is always good." Yes, it is his nature.

When the priest tells us rather bluntly to "Go," at the end of Mass, I don't think of getting on with what is "real" in life now that a "ritual" is over. Mass is both a completion and a first step. A completion, because of the very real encounter with God who has blessed, forgiven, accepted, instructed, and filled me with himself. Nothing can ever undo what one Mass, each and every one, has done in and for me.

When the priest says "Go" it is also a first step as to what I will be and do in the hours and days ahead. I have never liked the idea of an hour a week for God. If God is worth anything, he is worth every hour. He is worth everything. At one point in my adult life I remembered the morning offering we said as children in school and began to say it again at the beginning of each day.

"O Jesus, through the Immaculate Heart of Mary, I offer You my prayers, works, joys, and sufferings of this day in union with the Holy Sacrifice of the Mass throughout the world. . . ." (Apostleship of Prayer)

Once again, as in the Mass itself—when the people offer gifts of themselves, joined to the perfect gift of Christ—here was a reminder to me to offer myself in every way, every day. On the one hand, I began to orient my entire goal in life to Christ in sort of the big ways; and on the other, to try to make every little thing worthy to be included in the morning offering.

While the morning offering is an aid to what I want to accomplish; the grace to do so comes from God alone. My stumbling block is always myself, and my failures almost always have to do with a lapse of love. His grace is sometimes, and more and more often, evident to me, as I stop at moments and see where I can do a better job in living out my morning offering.

Sometimes the priest says another dismissal prayer:
"Go in peace to love and serve the Lord."

When I retired, a new way of serving the Lord opened up to me when Father Kevin asked me to bring Holy Communion to homebound people. I began to get names of Catholics unable to go to Mass on account of illness or some incapacity, people who had requested that Holy Communion be brought to them at home, usually once a month and in some cases every week. Barbara and John were the first people I visited, and they wanted it every week.

Barbara had had multiple sclerosis for about ten years and John was suffering from lung and brain cancer. He was Barbara's caregiver until he became ill himself—and then he continued to help her get out of bed and put on her braces every day. That winter, they were always sitting side-by-side in a bay window when I came every week with Holy Communion. John was quiet but attuned to everything, putting in his opinion from time to time as I got to know them. As they were the first people to whom I brought the Eucharist, I had anticipated a short, pleasant exchange, then Holy Communion, leaving shortly after that. In their case, Barbara so loved conversation, and she expressed such immense faith and spiritual insight, that I was always drawn to spend more time with them.

Barbara said some astounding things: First, that her focus was always on Jesus crucified, and then, with a sweeping motion toward the crippled lower half of her body, that she offered all this to Jesus on the cross. Another day, after Communion prayers, she said that all she looked forward to now was to be at the heavenly supper—adding that, as at any banquet, she hopes to know people who are there.

It seemed I had known Barbara and John a long time, but in only three months John died. I was surprised to get a call from Barbara on a Sunday evening a few hours after his death. She wanted to thank me for having called the day before, on Saturday morning. She didn't know why I had called but considered it a "divine intervention." John was then in the hospital, dying, and she had seized upon my call to ask me to notify the hospital chaplain. That morning I woke up the Catholic chaplain who was on call, and he visited John a last time.

My original purpose in calling Barbara had been lost in the need of the moment. The reason had been to tell her that I was coming over to put on her braces. Her son-in-law had been doing it on weekdays and she hoped to give him a rest on weekends. Once before, with great difficulty, I had put on her braces and was a little apprehensive about doing it again. In the end, it was a favor of a spiritual kind she needed, and for Barbara—as for many Catholics—the visit of a priest to one's deathbed counted greatly. In knowing Barbara and John, and continuing to see Barbara in the years since John died, I began to know what my pastor meant when he told me that being a Eucharistic Minister would make a difference in my own life.

What have I learned from Barbara and John? That so often both husband and wife become unable to take care of each other. That they can keep on going, keep on giving, keep on loving, and keep on praying through it all. That out the other side comes redemption, that mysterious saving of the soul. Barbara is one of my models for this. Out of her debilitating illness, loss of her husband, and then loss of her three-generation home, she has found a new calling. Like everyone, Barbara fought giving up her home as long as she could, but she made a good transition to assisted living.

Other residents are often puzzled as to why she is so happy despite being crippled by multiple sclerosis. She tells one and all who it is who makes her happy. Some people back off at first, perceiving her to be too religious for their taste, but—when people witness real joy—they bend before it. In Barbara I see someone personally chosen by God, out of her long servanthood and dedicated suffering, to do something more for him in this life. To bring more faith, hope, and love to her new friends in assisted living.

For Barbara, I think every day is a good day. For her, as for the Africans on their way to Mass, the Lord is always good. There is certainly a niche for Barbara in my personal Communion of Saints, my friends who lead me to God.

On a typical Sunday, I approach the tabernacle just as the recessional hymn is over and people are filing out of the church. My plan is always to go directly to the homebound people, bearing the just-consecrated Sacred Host for them to partake of with our community. In this way, the ill are remembered at a time when they are on the outside, like the ten lepers who stood apart and called out, "Jesus Master, have pity on us." The ill know on whom to call for true healing, and they are uplifted by Jesus who hears their cries and comes to them from out of his great sacrifice, which we—and he—relive in the Mass.

I know he hears my cry. All of us are crying, all the world is crying until our tears are turned into joy. An archaic meaning of joy is glad praise or worship, and, even now, joy is something that comes to me in surprising ways. I cannot seek joy, only wait for it as I do for God. And as I wait, I am before the Lord who sees me in all the stages of my life, and I say to him:

Here I am, Lord, a long-awaited first child in the arms of my parents at my Baptism. Here I am, an excited second-grader at the Communion rail for the first time. Here I am, a college student—not so interested in you. Here I am, a grieving mother, waiting in my hospital bed for Holy Communion. Here I am, busy in a career, going to Mass with my blind father. Here I am, next to my husband, writing these words.

May my life, Lord, like the Mass in my life, be eternally in your presence.

Deo Gratias.

EPILOGUE
LATIN MASS REVISITED

"Grant that . . . we may be made partakers of his divinity . . ."
"Deus qui humanae"
Saint Andrew Daily Missal, 1956

A bulletin board announcement of a month of Latin Masses caught my eye one day. The Masses were to be offered on Saturday afternoons in October in Bradford, Vermont, about thirty miles from my home. And so on the first Saturday I drove north on a warm fall afternoon to see what it was all about.

At the outset, the pastor told us this would be his first Mass said in Latin since 1967—forty years ago—and that he was a bit rusty. He recommended that we use a 1962 Missal and offered to order a supply for us. Many people had brought their own assorted, vintage missals. Mostly older people were present, but a good number of young including whole families were there as well. The church was about two-thirds full.

In those forty years of which the priest spoke, I had been present at only a few Latin Masses. The first was at Aquinas House at Dartmouth College, where presumably it was offered primarily to give students a chance to attend one for the first time. It was sparsely attended, and the priest told the largely older congregation that we should not be there out of nostalgia. I had not even imagined such a thing and so felt a little insulted; however, it was a fair warning that such feelings can be at play and are not proper. Again, in Rome in 2000, I heard the Latin Mass twice in the Bernini chapel of St. Peter's Basilica, where it was said every day at 5:00 in the afternoon.

On this day in Vermont, I desired the quiet dignity and solemn mystery which I remembered about the Latin Mass from my early years. I don't believe this is nostalgia, only a recognition of the quality of the form of something that happens to be old. The startup of this Latin Mass in an ordinary parish—with a promise by the pastor to offer it regularly if it was well-attended—was obviously a response to Pope Benedict XVI's apostolic letter of 2007, Motu Proprio Data," in which he says:

"Let the Missale Romanum promulgated by Paul VI be
held as the ordinary expression of the 'law of prayer' of the
Catholic Church of the Latin Rite. But let the Missale
Romanum promulgated by St. Pius V and published anew
by Bl. John XXIII be held as the extraordinary expression
of the same 'law of prayer' of the Church and let it enjoy due
honor on account of its venerable and ancient use."

In other words, the "new" Mass continues to be the ordinary Mass of the Church. The Latin Mass, for which the last missal was prepared in 1962, may be celebrated as the extraordinary Mass wherever the faithful desire it, without the necessity of the local bishop's permission.

On this day I was in for some surprises. First, the priest and his server, a deacon, said the prayers of the Mass in Latin almost as if they had not taken a break of forty years. Second, the people themselves spoke right up in their own responses, few though they are, to the priest. The helpfulness of a missal for the Latin Mass was brought home to me, not that I ever doubted it. I was glad to have my *Saint Andrew Daily Missal* from 1956. It was perfect. The *Missal* precedes our modern use of the three cycles of readings, so on this 19th Sunday after Pentecost, there were the same Epistle and Gospel and other Proper prayers as had been used on this day at least forty years ago, perhaps as long ago as four hundred years.

I found myself doing what I described in an early chapter on my childhood. I followed the Mass by listening for the priest's first words of each prayer in Latin, and then I continued reading them either in Latin, or in English on the opposite page—whichever worked best. All these years people have been debating the relative merits of Latin and English in the Mass, so I was surprised to realize that a better debate may be on the merits of the English translation of the Latin Mass vis a vis the English of the new Mass. The *English* translation of the Latin Mass is beautiful and theologically awesome, and in some places fairly different from the present-day Mass in English.

One example appeared during the Offertory—a time of the Mass when the priest quietly prepares the altar and prays over the offerings. I have always been drawn in to the Offertory of the Mass, wanting to follow the priest as he uncovers the chalice, places a host on the paten, pours water and wine into the chalice, washes his hands, and offers the bread and wine. It is true that there is a drawback in that these actions are not so easily visible when the priest faces the high altar in the Latin Mass. However, it is more important to be aware of them and to follow them with the mind and heart, and the ears and lips, than to actually see them. In one such moment, while saying the Offertory prayers in my missal, I discovered—or rediscovered—the prayer that the priest says when he mixes water and wine in the chalice. My *Saint Andrew Daily Missal* says that the mixing of water and wine is a symbol of the union of Christ with Christians. It begins *"Deus, qui humanae..."*:

"O God, who in a wonderful manner created and ennobled human nature and still more wonderfully renewed it; grant that, by the mystery of this water and wine, we may be made partakers of His Divinity who was pleased to become partaker of our humanity, Jesus Christ, Your Son, our Lord, who being God, lives and reigns with You in the unity of the Holy Spirit, forever and ever. Amen."

"Partake" is such a fine word. Dictionary meanings of "partake" are: "to eat or drink some," "to take or have a share," or "to have to some extent the nature or character of." Not all, the definition reminds me. Just some. Whatever God gives. Whatever I can properly take. In a Eucharistic setting, it is a finer word than "share," a more common word used for everything from toys, to rooms, to books, to meals.

Perhaps I have only just begun to understand why the priest mixes water with wine in the chalice just before he offers the wine. Water is the sacramental sign of our restored and uplifted humanity in Baptism, in which we are reborn into Christ. St. Paul thought that going into the water, we participate in the death of Christ and that coming out of it, we participate in his resurrection.

Thus far in the Mass, I have been a participant. I have gone down into the water. I have offered myself and the work of my human hands, as I have joined in the sacrifice of Christ. Now I am on a threshold, recalling my coming out of the baptismal water as a new creation. When water is mixed with wine in the Eucharist, it is commingled with the sign of the humanity of Christ, and when this wine, the sign of his human blood, is consecrated and I consume it, I partake of his divinity—inseparable now from his humanity.

I have never aspired to divinity. I hold onto my humanity tenaciously. In fact, I want to be human. The good thing for me is that I always will be, even when God "grants" that I partake of him. These words of St. Cyril of Jerusalem take me to the next step:

> "Therefore with full assurance let us partake of the body
> and blood of Christ. For in the figure of bread you are given
> His body, and in the figure of wine His blood, that when
> you partake of the body and blood of Christ, you become
> one body with Him and one blood with Him. For thus do
> we become Christ-bearers, since His body and blood are
> diffused through our members. Thus, according to Blessed
> Peter, do we become 'sharers in the divine nature' (2 Pet
> 1:4)."

And so in something as quiet as the mixing of the water and wine, a prayer of the Latin Mass reveals Christ all the more fully. I unexpectedly gain something from an older prayer—even one word translated from an older prayer. I will think a lot more about the word "partake," because it points me in a way I could not choose, on my own, to go.

Rosemary Lunardini

REFERENCES

Missals: The Prayers of the Mass in this book are from the author's personal collection of missals listed in order of their use.

Pray Always. Rev. Alphonse Sausen, O.S.B. Catholic Book Publishing Co. 1936.

Saint Joseph Sunday Missal. Rev. Hugo H. Hoever, S.O. Cist., Ph.D. Catholic Book Publishing Co.1957-1953. (Scripture readings are from *Confraternity Edition of the Old and New Testament*. Confraternity of Christian Doctrine (CCD). Washington, D.C.)

Saint Andrew Daily Missal. Dom Gaspar Lefebvre, O.S.B., et al. Saint Andrew's Priory, Inc. Valyermo, Calif. 1956. Published by E.M. Lohman Co. Saint Paul, Minn. 1957. (Scripture readings are from *Confraternity Edition*, cited above.) Collect, Introit, and Gospel from the Burial Mass, and Gradual from the Nuptial Mass used with permission of Saint Andrew's Priory.

Saint Andrew Bible Missal. Translated and adapted from *Missel Dominical de l'assemblee*. Benedictines of Saint-Andre d'Ottignies.1981. Excerpts from the English translation of *The Roman Missal*, ICEL 1973. Published by William J. Herten Co., Inc., Brooklyn, N.Y.1982.

Magnificat. Excerpts from the English translation of the Order of the Mass from *The Roman Missal*. ICEL. 1973. Excerpts from the *New American Bible with Revised New Testament and Psalms*. CCD. 1970, 1986, 1991. Published by Magnificat USA LLC. Yonkers, N.Y. 1998-2008.

Bibles and Commentaries: Scripture selections, including those of the Mass, are from the following bibles listed in order of their use.

The Family Rosary Commemorative Edition of the Catholic Bible. Confraternity Version. Ed. Rev. John P. O'Connell. CCD. 1957-50. Published by The Catholic Press Inc. Chicago. 1957.

The New American Bible. CCD. Washington, D.C. 1970, 1986, 1991. Published by Oxford University Press. 2004.

Other Sources:

Barclay, William. *The Gospel of John.* Rev. Ed. Westminster Press. Philadelphia. 1975.

Bell, John A. "The Summons." *RitualSong.* GIA Publications, Inc. Chicago. 1996.

Benedict XVI. *"Motu Proprio Data."* Apostolic Letter of July 7, 2007.

Catechism of the Catholic Church, 2nd Edition. United States Catholic Conference.

Libreria Editrice Vaticana. Citta del Vaticano. 1997.

Claudel, Paul. *I Believe in God.* Ignatius Press. San Francisco, Calif. 2002.

McKarns, Rev. James. *Go Tell Everyone.* Alba House. New York, N.Y. 1985.

McKenzie, John L., S.J. *Dictionary of the Bible.* Macmillan Publishing Co., Inc. 1965.

Mork, Dom Wulstan, O.S.B. *Transformed by Grace, Scripture, Sacraments & the Sonship of Christ.* Servant Books. Cincinnati, Ohio. 2004. (Quote of St. Cyril of Jerusalem reprinted by permission of St. Anthony Messenger Press, 28 W. Liberty St., Cincinnati, Ohio 45202.)

Nouwen, Henri. *With Burning Hearts: A Meditation on the Eucharist.* Orbis Books. 2003.

Kelley, J.N.D. Oxford Dictionary of Popes. Oxford University Press. 1986.

Hallett, Elaine. Unpublished notes "On living the liturgical year."

Printed in the United States
By Bookmasters